The Artist and The Child

THE ARTIST & THE CHILD

Exhibition of Children's Books
and Original Illustrations from the
John D. Merriam Collection

BOSTON, TRUSTEES OF THE PUBLIC LIBRARY
OF THE CITY OF BOSTON, 1980

ACKNOWLEDGMENTS

The Boston Public Library expresses appreciation to the following Associates and Staff who have contributed to the research, organization, and publication of this catalogue: Sinclair H. Hitchings, Jane Manthorne, Laura V. Monti, Priscilla Moulton, Richard N. Zonghi, and the staff of the Fine Arts Department. Special appreciation is extended to John D. Merriam for sharing his knowledge and collection for the exhibition and this catalogue.

Library of Congress Cataloging in Publication Data

The Artist and the child.

   Catalog of an exhibition held at the Boston Public Library, Sept. 21-Dec. 31, 1980.
   1. Illustrated books, Children's — Exhibitions. 2. Merriam, John D. — Art collections — Exhibitions. 3. Illustrators — Biography. I. Boston. Public Library.
NC965.A77   741.64'2'074014461   80-21086
ISBN 0-89073-065-2

Designed by Richard Zonghi

Printed by The Thomas Todd Company,
Boston, Massachusetts

COVER

Boris Artzybasheff. Dust jacket design for *Herodotus, the First European Historian*, edited by Gordon King.

FRONTISPIECE

Vera Bock. ". . . there on one step stood a chest." Illustration for *A Ring and a Riddle* by M. Ilin and E. Segal.

Contents

Foreword

In line with its long tradition of offering changing experiences in the study and appreciation of art, the Boston Public Library served as site for THE ARTIST AND THE CHILD, an Exhibition of Children's Books and Original Illustrations from the collection of John D. Merriam, from September 21 to December 31, 1980. It is appropriate that a library significant for its permanent art and architecture serve also as center for a changing sequence of art shows. Thus, down the years the Boston Public Library has mounted major exhibitions from its own and private collections — the works of such artists as Clare Leighton, Thomas Nason, Fritz Eichenberg, and others.

THE ARTIST AND THE CHILD reflects more than forty years of collecting by John D. Merriam. In the course of his pursuit of fine books and original art he has focused principally on fantasy, the imagination, the inner world of dreams and visions. Whether a book or drawing was created for children or adults has been of no consequence to him as collector. Personal taste and interest in art as art have dominated his choices. That many items in his collection are defined or categorized as works for children is accidental or, rather, coincidental with his delight and preoccupation with the fantastic and surreal.

Among the original drawings and watercolors as well as books in this exhibition there is breadth of mood and subject and style. There are sentiment and whimsy, boldness and delicacy, elegance and simplicity, motion and quietude. There are minor traumas like a boy trapped in an umbrella stand; and major ones like a child caught on the blade of a windmill. There are children who look like bees — and a lady who resembles a lion. There are horses that prance and bound and — of course — fly. The presence of lyre and dulcimer and pipe in several pictures suggests that the exhibition is played to music. Throughout, however, it is fantasy, consistent with the collector's preference in art, which dominates the exhibition.

The art shown here came from the brushes and pens of distinguished artists as well as more obscure practitioners. In his collecting John D. Merriam focused on art rather than on artist. He brought together the works of relatively unknown illustrators like Emma Troth and D. Emerson and those of widely acknowledged artists like Arthur Rackham, Maxfield Parrish, Boris Artzybasheff. Consequently, an important aspect of this exhibition is its invitation to viewers to discover — as did the collector — the range of orginality and imagination in the work of obscure as well as recognized artists.

The Boston Public Library invites viewers of THE ARTIST AND THE CHILD and users of this catalogue to share any additional data they may have about the art and the artists included. In this way the advancement of knowledge remains a continuing process — and art itself becomes a continuing discovery.

PHILIP J. MCNIFF
Director and Librarian
Boston Public Library

Catalogue Guide

This catalogue of the John D. Merriam exhibition is arranged alphabetically by artist. Each item exhibited is numbered. Each item illustrated is so noted at the end of its descriptive entry. Each artist's works are arranged alphabetically by titles of exhibited items, except that, when two or more works are illustrations for the same publication, the arrangement is in order of appearance in the published work. When both a book and original art for that book are shown in the exhibition, the book entry precedes the entry for the original art.

Each book in the exhibition is fully described. In addition to imprint data of place, publisher, and date, the following information is provided: pagination, height in centimeters, description of binding and dust jacket and, where applicable, a note on limited edition. Data on books not shown in the exhibit are given in an abbreviated form: author, title, place, publisher, date. Information enclosed in brackets — usually date, place of publication, or pagination — represents data determined by the exhibit staff.

Descriptive data for original art are given in this order: medium, caption, date (when known), and dimensions in inches (height preceding width). Captions in quotation marks represent actual titles assigned to their pictures by the illustrators, or (when such titles are not provided) appropriate descriptions quoted from the books. Captions not in quotation marks were supplied by the exhibit staff.

Child! do not throw this book about;
    Refrain from the unholy pleasure
Of cutting all the pictures out!
    Preserve it as your chiefest treasure.
       . . .

And when your prayers complete the day,
    Darling, your little tiny hands
Were also made, I think, to pray
    For men that lose their fairylands.

Hilaire Belloc
*The Bad Child's Book
of Beasts* (1896)

Artists

Boris Artzybasheff 1899-1965

Born in Kharkov, Russia. His father, M. P. Artsybashev, was a distinguished novelist. He studied art at the Prince Tenisheff School in St. Petersburg. In the revolution of 1918 he served five months in the White Army, then left Russia as a seaman and in 1919 arrived in New York. He worked first making ornaments and lettering in an engraver's shop; he drew caricatures for the *New York World*, designed women's clothes, painted murals in 1922 for a restaurant, designed stage sets for Michael Fokine's Russian ballet, and, also in 1922, illustrated a book published by Alfred A. Knopf. From this first commission he went on to become a virtuoso book designer and prominent illustrator, with special influence in the realm of children's books. For *Poor Shaydullah* (1931) and *Seven Simeons* (1937) he created text as well as pictures and pointed the way toward children's books which in our time often have been both written and illustrated by a single person. In the twenties in New York he met a contemporary from Russia, Vera Bock, who became a longstanding friend and notable compatriot in the realm of book illustration. After 1940 he was chiefly occupied as one of the leading commercial artists of his generation. His work included more than two hundred *Time Magazine* covers and major advertising designs for Ford, General Motors, and other corporations.

Scratchboard drawings, possibly unpublished, illustrating *Adventures of Don Quixote de la Mancha* by Miguel de Cervantes Saavedra, as follows:

1 Don Quixote slashing at wine sacks, 10½″ x 8″.
2 Don Quixote tilting at windmills, 10¼″ x 8¼″.
3 Sancho tossed in a blanket by people at the inn, 10¼″ x 8″.
4 Don Quixote on ground, challenged by knight on horseback, 9¼″ x 7¼″.

5 *Aesop's Fables.* Edited and illustrated with Wood Engravings by Boris Artzybasheff. New York, The Viking Press, 1933.

83p. 23.5cm. Red cloth binding, onlaid paper with black and yellow design. Dust jacket printed in red and black on beige.

Proofs of wood engravings in black and white illustrating *Aesop's Fables*, as follows:

6 "The Hare and the Tortoise," p. 31, 4½″ x 4½″. (illus.)

7 "The Tiger and the Bulls," p. 35, 7″ x 4½″.
8 "The Ass in the Lion's Skin," p. 41, 4½″ x 4½″.
9 "The Ass and the Little Dog," p. 57, 7″ x 4½″.
10 "The Horse and the Ass," p. 61, 4½″ x 4½″.
11 "The Peacock and the Crane," p. 77, 7″ x 4½″.
12 "The Lion, the Tiger, and the Fox," p. 80, 4½″ x 4½″.

Brush drawings illustrating *The Apple Tree* by Margery Williams Bianco (New York, George H. Doran Co., 1926), as follows:

13 Design for half title, 9″ x 5¾″. (illus.)
14 Sheet of four initial letters, 5″ x 7″.

Illustrations for *The Circus of Dr. Lao* by Charles G. Finney (New York, The Viking Press, 1935), as follows:

15 Black watercolor design for dust jacket, 18½″ x 14″.
16 Pencil, black watercolor, and white brush or pen study for illustration, "A Lecture on *Lusus Naturae*," p. 30, 16½″ x 10″. (illus.)

17 *Creatures* by Padraic Colum. With Drawings by Boris Artzybasheff. New York, The Macmillan Co., 1927.

56p. 23.5cm. Green paper on boards, design in black, cloth back. Dust jacket printed in red and black repeating the binding design.

Black watercolors illustrating *Creatures*, as follows:

18 Jackdaw, p. 13, 17″ x 12″.
19 Crows, p. 15, 17″ x 12″.
20 Monkeys, p. 37, 17″ x 12″.
21 Bison, p. 39, 17″ x 12″.
22 Snake, p. 41, 16½″ x 11¾″. (illus.)
23 Fish, p. 43, 14¾″ x 10¾″.
24 Vulture, p. 51, 16½″ x 12″.

25 *The Fairy Shoemaker and Other Fairy Poems.* Illustrated by Boris Artzybasheff. New York, The Macmillan Co., 1928.

114p. 22cm. Green cloth binding with stripes of yellow, gold, and green. Dust jacket printed in green and black on yellow.

Scratchboard drawings illustrating *The Fairy Shoemaker*, as follows:

26 "With a bridge of white mist Columbkill he crosses, on his stately journeys," p. 41, 7″ x 5½″.
27 The gnomies, playing faint music in the wood, p. 59, 7½″ x 5½″. (illus.)
28 "There was an old woman went blackberry picking," p. 67, 7¼″ x 5½″.
29 "Where the sea-snakes coil and twine," p. 89, 7″ x 5½″.

Black watercolors illustrating *Feats on the Fjord* by Harriet Martineau (New York, The Macmillan Co., 1924), as follows:

30 Pictorial endpapers, 10⅜″ x 9¾″.

31 Initial letters, 9½″ x 9½″.

32 "A Fellow Who Looks as if He Did Not Like His Business," p. 21, 10½″ x 7½″.

33 Chapter heading depicting snooping fox, p. 33, 8¼″ x 9¾″.

34 "Now I can say I have seen Nipen," p. 39, 10¼″ x 7¼″. (illus.)

35 "A reindeer stood on the ridge," p. 179, 10½″ x 7½″.

36 "I do so very much want to fly abroad, just for once, over the fjord," p. 201, 10½″ x 7½″.

37 *The Forge in the Forest* by Padraic Colum with Pictures by Boris Artzybasheff. New York, The Macmillan Co., 1925.

148p. 19cm. Yellow cloth binding stamped in green and blue. Dust jacket printed in red, black, and green on cream.

Black watercolors illustrating *The Forge in the Forest*, as follows:

38 Title page and opposite (with pencil), 10¾″ x 16¼″.

39 "Plunging and plunging, the horses went farther and farther off their course," pp. 28-29, 9½″ x 16″. (illus.)

40 "The seven stood on the side of the mountain and blessed the people," pp. 88-89, 10″ x 15″.

41 "Solomon made him gaze upon his ring," pp. 100-101, 9¾″ x 15″.

42 " 'Go on, go on, your reverence,' said the goatherd," pp. 124-125, 10¼″ x 15¾″.

43 *Ghond the Hunter* by Dhan Gopal Mukerji. Illustrated by Boris Artzybasheff. New York, E. P. Dutton & Co., 1928.

204p. 20.5cm. Orchid color cloth binding stamped in gold. Dust jacket printed in black and white on yellow.

Black watercolors illustrating *Ghond the Hunter*, as follows:

44 Dust jacket design, 8″ x 7¾″.

45 Benji, the pet mongoose, p. 168, 8½″ x 8½″. (illus.)

46 Mita the cat on a branch of a mango tree, p. 174, 8½″ x 8½″.

Scratchboard drawings illustrating *Herodotus, the First European Historian* edited by Gordon King (Garden City, N. Y., Doubleday, 1929), as follows:

47 Dust jacket design, black and red, 9½″ x 13¼″. (cover)

48 "Homer and Hesiod were the poets who first gave distinctive names to the gods and described their forms," chapter 3, 6″ x 4½″. (illus).

49 "Tame animals would be still more numerous were it not for what happens to cats. When a fire breaks out a wonderful thing happens to these animals," chapter 3, 4½″ x 4½″.

50 "There was among the leaders one extraordinary commander, a woman, Artemisia. She went into war more for the glory of it than anything else," chapter 8, 4½″ x 4½″.

51 "When I consider how short is all human life pity enters my heart. Rich in numbers as my armies may be, who of them all will be alive an hundred years from now?" chapter 8, 4½″ x 4½″.

Black watercolors illustrating *Little Brother Francis of Assisi* by Michael Williams (New York, The Macmillan Co., 1926), as follows:

52 "My brother, God give you peace," frontispiece, 17¼″ x 9″.

53 Francis kissed the hand of the beggar, p. 28, 17″ x 9″.

54 Francis came into the presence of the sultan, p. 124, 17½″ x 11″.

55 "The far sweeter music of heaven," p. 172, 17½″ x 11″. (illus.)

56 *Magic Strings; Marionette Plays* with Production Notes by Remo Bufano. Decorations by Boris Artzybasheff. New York, The Macmillan Co., 1939.

182p. 20cm. Peach color cloth binding printed in black. Dust jacket printed in orange and black on pale lavender.

Black watercolors illustrating *Magic Strings*, as follows:

57 Dust jacket design, 14″ x 11″. (illus.)

58 The Three Partners, p. 79, 11½″ x 9″.

Scratchboard drawings on celluloid illustrating *Orpheus, Myths of the World* by Padraic Colum (New York, The Macmillan Co., 1930), as follows:

59 Indian, p. 214, 15″ x 10¾″. (illus.)

60 Zuni, p. 310, 12″ x 10″.

61 *Poor Shaydullah* told and illustrated by Boris Artzybasheff. New York, The Macmillan Co., 1931.

[59]p. 21.5cm. Gray cloth binding stamped in black. Dust jacket printed in red and black on cream.

Scratchboard drawings illustrating *Poor Shaydullah*, as follows:

62   Shaydullah and the Lion, 16″ x 16½″.

63   Shaydullah and the Banana Tree, 15½″ x 16½″. (illus).

64   Shaydullah and the Fish, 15″ x 13½″.

65   Shaydullah and the Monsters, Demons and Devas of the Wild Tempest, 14½″ x 25½″.

66   Allah and his Angels Appearing to Shaydullah, 17″ x 29½″.

67   *Seven Simeons; A Russian Tale* Retold and Illustrated by Boris Artzybasheff. New York, The Viking Press, 1937.

[31]p. 28.5cm. Green cloth binding with blind stamped design. Dust jacket printed in gold, red, black, and green on cream.

Watercolor studies for dust jacket design of *Seven Simeons*, as follows:

68   15½″ x 12″. (illus.)

69   11¼″ x 8¼″.

70   11¼″ x 8½″.

71   Black watercolor, "The King's huntsmen blew their horns loud, the King's horsemen came galloping out, and King Douda rode forth to hunt . . . ," second full-page illustration for *Seven Simeons*, 10½″ x 8¼″.

72   *Three and the Moon; Legendary Stories of Old Brittany, Normandy and Provence.* Stories told by Jacques Dorey and illustrated by Boris Artzybasheff. New York, Alfred A. Knopf, 1929.

103p. 25.5cm. Blue cloth binding stamped in silver. Dust jacket printed in black, red, silver, and purple on white.

Scratchboard drawings illustrating *Three and the Moon*, as follows:

73   Heading for Contents page, 5″ x 5″.

74   Heading for Prologue, p. 3, 5¾″ x 5¾″.

75   Heading for "The Story of Ivon Tortik," p. 11, 4″ x 5½″.

76   The Vouivre, the serpent with diamond claws, p. 86, 11¾″ x 8¾″. (illus.)

77   Taulat de Rugimon, master and lord of the mountain, astride his horse, p. 96, 9¾″ x 7¼″.

Black watercolors illustrating *Verotchka's Tales* by Mamin-Siberiak (New York, E. P. Dutton & Co., 1922), as follows:

78   Endpaper design, 15″ x 12″.

79   Initial letters, 7″ x 11″.

80   "Long, long did the unfortunate rabbit run. It seemed to him that the wolf was right behind him," p. 9, 13″ x 9″.

81   " 'Why, aren't they all mine, the sun and the grass and the flowers!' 'No, pardon me. They are all mine,' said a fuzzy caterpillar . . . ," p. 17, 12½″ x 9″.

82   "In a word, there was a row," p. 55, 12¾″ x 9⅛″. (illus.)

83   "When he rests, he sits on the very edge of the roof, eats his piece of bread for lunch, while I pick up the crumbs," p. 67, 10½″ x 7¼″.

84   *The Wonder-Smith and His Son; A Tale from the Golden Childhood of the World*, Retold by Ella Young. Illustrated by Boris Artzybasheff. New York, Longmans, Green & Co., 1927.

189p. 21cm. Green cloth binding stamped in gold. Dust jacket printed in black and green on ivory.

Black watercolors illustrating *The Wonder-Smith and His Son*, as follows:

85   Initial letters, 11½″ x 21½″.

86   "My blessing to you, brother of mine; white love of running water," p. 35, 16½″ x 11″.

87   "Our king bespeaks your help. Behold the gifts and tokens of Balor," p. 65, 17″ x 11½″. (illus.)

88   "I am Hrut of the many shapes, the son of Sruth, the son of Sru," p. 77, 16¾″ x 11″.

89   "Balor's devastating eye was close shut. Hugely the eyelid weighed upon it," p. 91, 16¾″ x 11″.

90   "A Dune with courts and passages and secret chambers," pp. 104-105, 16¾″ x 23¼″.

91   "Wye-Hoo! Wye-Hoo! Wye-Hoo! Bal-a-loo! Bal-a-loo! Ai! Ai! Ai!" pp.122-123, 16½″ x 23½″.

92   "Let us leave this rhyming," said the Djinn. "It is fit only for women. Show me a Wonder-Feat," p. 137, 16½″ x 12″.

93   "He saw that it was the great Piast herself, drawn fold on fold from the deep," pp. 180-181, 16¾″ x 23¼″.

MISCELLANY: Designs by Artzybasheff for Christmas cards, magazine covers, books not identified, and other purposes, as follows:

94   Wood engraving, "Bliss" (the Santa Claus family), 9¾″ x 6¾″. (illus).

95   Wood engraving, "Christmas 1931" (view of sad Santa and weeping reindeer), 8⅜″ x 6½″.

96   Black watercolor, shrouded figure with torch, 13″ x 9¾″.

97   Black watercolor, wolf clashing with knight, 12½″ x 9½″.

98   Black watercolor, boy restraining snarling wolf by scruff of neck, 12¾″ x 9¾″.

99   White watercolor on black paper, "Kittyfly," 9″ x 11″. (illus.)

100   Cliche verre (an experimental technique of drawing on glass and then printing as from a photographic negative), three fantastic humanoid creatures, one presenting flower to another while a third peers from behind a tree, 19¼″ x 14″.

101 Watercolor and gold paint, cover design (astrologer-sorcerer making flower grow in snow) for *The Golden Book Magazine*, February 1929, 16″ x 11¾″.

102 Pencil drawing, study for "Children's Spring Book Festival," Sunday supplement, *New York Herald Tribune*, May 7, 1939, 13″ x 11″.

Costume designs in watercolor, as follows:

103 Wolf fancily garbed in gold boots, cape, and feathered hat, 21″ x 14¾″.

104 Ballerina with angel wings, 18″ x 10½″.

105 Child dressed as red elf, 14″ x 10½″.

106 Girl in Russian costume, 18½″ x 13″.

107 Two dancing children dressed as rabbits, 11¼″ x 16″.

108 Two children in costume, 15¼″ x 11½″.

109 Wolf disguised as Russian peasant woman coming home from market, 17½″ x 14½″.

110 Costumed figure of man with dueling pistol, 19½″ x 13″.

111 Gouache drawings, strips of chapter headings (subjects ranging from microscopic views to wild animals), mounted and framed as a single picture, 28″ x 18″.

Sheets of pen-drawn initial letters for *Hecatean County* (book not located), measurements as follows:

112 7¼″ x 7¼″.

113 7¾″ x 10½″.

Edmund Birckhead Bensell
1842-

Born in Philadelphia. He was a painter, illustrator, and engraver. He was the brother of the painter George Frederick Bensell, who was his teacher. Later he studied at the Pennsylvania Academy of Fine Arts. In addition to illustrating various stories and books, he made forty designs for an edition of Shakespeare.

114 Pencil drawing, "Davy falls into the elastic spring," 11¼″ x 8″. Illustration for "Davy and the Goblin" by Charles E. Carryl (*St. Nicholas*, March 1885, p. 339). (illus.)

Reginald Bathurst Birch
1856-1943

Born in London. He came to the United States at the age of sixteen but later returned to Europe to study in Munich and Paris. He did many illustrations for *St. Nicholas* which are remarkable for their understanding and illumination of character and scene.

115 Gouache drawing, "Gaily the troubadour touched the guitar," 20⅝″ x 12⅜″. Illustration, p. 145, *Little Men* by Louisa May Alcott (Boston, Little, Brown & Co., 1901). (illus.)

116 Gouache drawing, 14″ x 11¼″. Frontispiece illustrating "In Christmas Season, Long Ago," a poem by Helen Gray Cone (*St. Nicholas*, December 1886). (illus.)

117 Pen drawing, "Sir Peter caught the pirate, and he took him by the neck," 18″ x 19½″. Illustration for "The Admiral's Caravan" by Charles E. Carryl (*St. Nicholas*, January 1892, p. 170).

118 Pen drawing, "Some bold bad thieves in a cave laughed out . . . ." Illustration for "Just for Fun" by Malcolm Douglas (*St. Nicholas*, March 1893, p. 360). (illus.)

119 Gouache drawing, "Three elves sailed forth on a flake of snow," 9¾″ x 15⅛″. Illustration for "The Cruise of the Elves," a poem by Felix Leigh (*St. Nicholas*, February 1893, p. 314).

120 Pen drawing, "Why, Boss!" exclaimed Dick, "Do you know him yourself?" 15″ x 16″. Illustration for "Little Lord Fauntleroy" by Frances Hodgson Burnett (*St. Nicholas*, August 1886, p. 736). (illus.)

Vera Bock

Born in St. Petersburg, Russia. Her mother was a concert pianist; her father, an international banker. She and her family were forced to flee the "mad upheaval" of the revolution, crossing Siberia into China, then on to San Francisco and New York. She returned to Europe in 1919 and for the next four years studied art on the continent and in England — such varied forms as wood engraving, illuminating, heraldry, printing, and photoengraving. On her return to the U. S. in 1923 she worked as a commercial artist. Among her varied activities were designing tapestries, interior decorating, producing murals, and restoring paintings. She began her career as an illustrator in 1929. In New York she met another Russian-American, Boris Artzybasheff, and the two artists became lifelong friends. In her long, active career as artist Vera Bock designed and illustrated numerous children's books and illustrated for *Coronet* and *Life Magazines*.

Watercolors illustrating *The Adventures of Maya the Bee* by Waldemar Bonsels (New York, Albert and Charles Boni, 1929), as follows:

121 Title page, 14″ x 8½″.

122 Single sheet of two chapter headings: "First Flight," p. 1; "The House of the Rose," p. 14; 12½″ x 8½″.

123 Single sheet of four chapter headings: "Alois, Ladybird and Poet," p. 163; "The Fortress," p. 172; "The Sentinel," p. 182; "The Warning," p. 194; 14″ x 18½″.

Illustrations for *Arabian Nights*, collected and edited by Andrew Lang (London, Longmans, Green & Co., 1946), as follows:

124 Watercolor, overlay for dust jacket, 12¾″ x 8¾″.

Black watercolor drawings, as follows:

125 Dust jacket, 13″ x 8¾″.

126 Frontispiece, 12″ x 9″.

127 "The Forty Thieves," p. 55, 12″ x 9″.

128 "Prince Ahmed and Fairy Paribanou," p. 69, 12″ x 9″.

129 "The Seven Voyages of Sindbad the Sailor," p. 143, 12″ x 9″.

130 "Prince Camaralzaman and Princess Badoura," p. 192, 12″ x 9″.

131 "Aladdin and the Wonderful Lamp," p. 209, 12″ x 9″. (illus.)

Black watercolor drawings illustrating *Birthday Candles Burning Bright; A Treasury of Birthday Poetry* selected by Sara and John E. Brewton (New York, The Macmillan Co., [1960]), as follows:

132 "So let thy Birthdays come to thee — Birthdays before seven," p. 39, 9″ x 7″. (illus.)

133 "So let thy Birthdays come to thee — Seven through Thirteen," p. 67, 8¾″ x 6¾″.

134 "Cakes and Candles," p. 83, 8¼″ x 7″.

135 *A Book-to-Begin-On, Magic People Around the World* by Barbara Softly. New York, Holt, Rinehart and Winston, [1970.]

[40]p. 22cm. Cloth binding printed in black, white, and brown. Dust jacket repeats binding design.

Black watercolor drawings, 10″ x 7″, illustrating *Bow Bells* by Katharine Gibson (New York, Longmans, Green and Co., 1943), as follows:

136 "Night Watch was sunning himself," p. 63. (illus.)

137 "Lame Simon could hear the cries of delight," p. 113.

138 *Bridled with Rainbows, Poems about Many things of Earth and Sky* selected by Sara and John E. Brewton. New York, The Macmillan Co., 1949.

191p. 24cm. Beige cloth binding stamped in black. Dust jacket printed in gold, blue, and black on white.

Black watercolor drawings for *Bridled with Rainbows*, as follows:

139 Dust jacket, 14″ x 11″.

140 Decoration, "Off to Somewhere," p. 1, 7¼″ x 6¼″. (illus.)

141 Decoration, "Deep in the Sky," p. 93, 8″ x 6¼″.

142 *Cinders* by Katharine Gibson. New York, Longmans, Green and Co., 1939.

132p. 20cm. Light yellow cloth binding stamped in red. Dust jacket printed in black and blue on yellow.

Black watercolor drawings for *Cinders*, as follows:

143 Sheet of decorations, 8½″ x 10½″.

144 Sheet of half-page illustrations for pages 77, 104, 105, 133, 9″ x 14″.

145 "The Surgeon Fell in with a Great Splash," p. 43, 10⅜″ x 8⅛″.

146 "Cinders Rode Flash Easily," p. 55, 10⅜″ x 8″. (illus.)

147 "Aye, It Will Surely Come True," p. 85, 10″ x 8″.

148 "He Had His Pipe, and There Were His Fiddlers Three," full page for p. 124; half-page illustration of Cinders standing next to golden coach, p. 125, both drawings on single sheet, 9″ x 13½″.

Graphite and black watercolor illustrations, 7½″ x 5″, for *A Cottage for Betsy* by Ruth Sawyer (New York, The Junior Literary Guild and Harper & Brothers, 1954), as follows:

149 Frontispiece, illustrating cottage. (illus.)

150 "That brought them creeping like ghosties around the corner of the house, standing stock-still, staring," p. 32.

151 ". . . she made up for it, dancing a merry reel around the table," p. 80.

Black watercolors illustrating *Cranes Flying South* by Nikolai N. Karazin (New York, Junior Literary Guild, Doubleday, Doran & Co., 1931), as follows:

152 Cover design, 14½″ x 12¼″.

153 "The golden dome of its churches," Chapter V, 10¼″ x 6⅝″.

154 "There was an unusually elegant howdah on its back," Chapter XX, 10½″ x 6¾″.

Black watercolor border decorations, 14¾″ x 10¾″, for *A Critical History of Children's Literature* by Cornelia Meigs and others (New York, The Macmillan Co., 1953), as follows:

155 Puss in Boots, Gulliver, Robinson Crusoe and

other literary figures, Part One, "Roots in the Past."

156   Alice in Wonderland, Little Women, and others, Part Two, "Widening Horizons."

157   Robin Hood, Long John Silver, Knights of the Round Table, and others, Part Three, "A Rightful Heritage."

Watercolors, 11½" x 5", illustrating *A Girl Who Would Be Queen; The Story and the Diary of the Young Countess Krasinska* by Eric P. Kelly and Clara Hoffmanowa (Chicago, A. C. McClurg & Co., 1939), as follows:

158   "Francoise's Diary," p. 33.

159   "Down through the years," p. 163.

160   *The Heroes; Greek Fairy Tales* by Charles Kingsley, illustrated by Vera Bock. New York, The Macmillan Co., [1954.]

193p. 21.5cm. Beige cloth binding stamped in brown. Dust jacket printed in blue, black, and peach on white.

Brush and pen drawings illustrating *The Heroes*, as follows:

161   ". . . put them into a great chest, and thrust them out to sea," p. 5, 9¼" x 7".

162   ". . . at last they put the hat upon his head," p. 29, 9¼" x 7".

163   ". . . Argus taught them to build a galley," p. 83, 9" x 7".

164   ". . . he must sow them with serpent's teeth, of which each tooth springs up into an armed man," p. 103, 9½" x 7¼". (illus.)

165   ". . . and castles high in air upon the cliffs," p. 125, 9¼" x 7".

Illustrations for *Jewels and Gems* by Lucile Saunders McDonald (New York, Thomas Y. Crowell Co., 1940), as follows:

166   Watercolor and gold paint overlay for dust jacket, 12" x 16¾".
Brush drawings in black watercolor, as follows:

167   Dust jacket (with some color), 12" x 17½".

168   Frontispiece, 11" x 8½".

169   Primitive man stringing a necklace of pearls, p. 12, 11" x 8¼".

170   Mythical creature with its tail encircling a diamond, p. 36, 11" x 8¼". (illus.)

171   Running figure with two boars, p. 128, 11" x 8½".

Brush drawings in black watercolor illustrating *Jock's Castle* by Katharine Gibson (New York, Longmans, Green & Co., 1940), as follows:

172   Pictorial endpapers, 11½" x 15¼".

173   "But I'm not often alone," p. 45, 11" x 8".

174   "From the road came a splintering sound," p. 53, 11" x 8¼". (illus.)

175   *King of the Cats* by Eileen O'Faolain with pictures by Vera Bock. New York, William Morrow & Co., 1942.

158p. 23.5cm. Yellow cloth binding with stamp design in blue. Dust jacket printed in green, blue, and black on gray.

Brush drawings illustrating *King of the Cats*, as follows:

176   "Kitty the Cat," p. 10, 10½" x 8".

177   "Adventures at the fair," p. 34, 9¾" x 7¾".

178   "In the White Knight's Mansion," p. 48, 10¾" x 8".

179   "The Night on the Fairy Mountain," p. 94, 10¾" x 8".

180   "Feast and Farewell," p. 144, 10¾" x 8". (illus.)

181   *Little Magic Horse, a Russian Tale* by Peter Ershoff. Translated by Tatiana Balkoff Drowne and Illustrated by Vera Bock. New York, The Macmillan Co., 1942.

[128]p. 26.5cm. Blue cloth binding. Dust jacket printed in pink, blue, black, and gold on white.

Watercolor illustrations for *Little Magic Horse*, as follows:

182   Dust jacket, 13" x 18½".

183   "But, alack, he had mounted front to back," 12½" x 8¼".

184   In the castle shed Daniel comes upon a homely pony with "bumps on his back like camel humps," 12½" x 8¼".

185   The villain grooms a steed while the knight, on the floor, watches, 12½" x 8¼".

186   The Firebird emerges in a flood of light, 12½" x 8¼".

187   The Princess plays her dulcimer, 12½" x 8¼".

188   The Wonder-Monster whale promises to help, 12½" x 8¼".

189   ". . . the red chest lands, dully clanking on the sands," 12½" x 8¼". (illus.)

190   Tzar and bride proceed hand in hand to church, 12½" x 8¼".

191   Sheet of four half-page designs, 13" x 17".

Brush drawings in black watercolor or black watercolor with brown, initial letters, vignettes, and spots for *Little Magic Horse*, 12½" x 8¼", as follows:

192   Sheet of seven.

193   Sheet of six.

Brush drawings in black watercolor for *Metten of Tyre* by Helena Carus (New York, Doubleday, Doran & Co., 1930), as follows:

194   Sheet of headings for 6 chapters (II - VII), 17" x 13¼".

195   "Melkarth made himself a golden cup so large that he could sit in the bottom of it," Chapter II, 12" x 8¼".

196 "They sang out a 'Ho, ho, ho' to each tread of their feet," Chapter III, 12½″ x 8¾″.

197 "For each bronze pot she gave a doeskin," Chapter V, 11½″ x 9″.

198 "He called to the molten metal," Chapter IX, 12″ x 8¼″.

199 "The proudest monument in the temple," Chapter X, 11½″ x 9″. (illus.)

200 *Nathaniel's Witch* by Katharine Gibson with pictures by Vera Bock. New York, Longmans, Green & Co., 1941.

136p. 23.5cm. Blue cloth binding with stars stamped in silver. Dust jacket printed in blue, black, and red on white.

Brush drawings in black watercolor illustrating *Nathaniel's Witch*, as follows:

201 Dust jacket, 12¾″ x 17½″.

202 Pictorial endpapers, 12¼″ x 8⅛″.

203 "The Pictures are for Peter," half-title, p. v (upper right); end piece, p. 136 (lower left), both on one sheet. 7⅜″ x 6″.

204 "A Witch in a Fog," half-title page, p. 21, 8⅜″ x 6″.

205 "Nathaniel eyed the bush wonderingly," p. 29, 10¾″ x 7¼″.

206 "Night after night this happened," p. 41, 10½″ x 7¼″.

207 "Nathaniel dashed the goblet to the ground," p. 45, 10¼″ x 7″. (illus.)

208 "Black Nick," p. 63, 6½″ x 5½″.

209 "The broom spread out in a long cometlike tail," p. 83, 10⅜″ x 5⅞″.

210 "Off the roof," p. 105, 6⅜″ x 5⅞″.

211 ". . . the toys," she declared, "had come down the chimney on a broomstick," p. 111, 10″ x 7¼″.

212 "Ever after," p. 121, 6½″ x 5½″.

213 "The house rang with their arguments," p. 131, 10⅜″ x 7¼″.

214 *The Oak Tree House* by Katharine Gibson with pictures by Vera Bock. New York, Longmans, Green & Co., 1936.

127p. 20cm. Yellow cloth binding with printed design in black. Dust jacket printed in blue and black on yellow.

Brush drawings in black watercolor for *The Oak Tree House*, as follows:

215 Title page and frontispiece, 11″ x 16½″.

216 Sheet of decorations, 9″ x 13½″.

217 "The Oak Tree house was finished," p. 45, 12¼″ x 8½″.

218 "Jock picked out the words slowly," p. 97, 9½″ x 8½″.

219 "The little king would not listen," p. 101, 10″ x 8½″. (illus.)

220 Piepowder or Dusty-Foot, from whom the Goodman bought the kerchief for the Dame, half-page, p. 114, 6½″ x 8½″.

221 *The Peacock Country* by P. Alston Waring decorated by Vera Bock. An Asia Book. New York, The John Day Co., [1948.]

100p. 24.5cm. Light gray cloth binding stamped in blue and gold. Dust jacket printed in black, pale green, and peach on white.

Brush and pen drawings in black watercolor heightened with white illustrating *The Peacock Country*, as follows:

222 Frontispiece, "Bowl of Rice," 13½″ x 9″.

223 Sheet of half titles: "Drubendra," p. 24; "The archery contest," p. 52; "The braggart," p. 28; "The prodigal," p. 4; "The friend of the elephant," p. 66; "Journey through Mourbhanj," p. 60; 9½″ x 14″.

224 Sheet of half titles: "The dancing fawn," p. 8; "The song of the Nagas," p. 96; "The lament of the cranes," p. 32; "The Lady of the Peacock Country," p. 70; "The farmer and the cobra," p. xii; "The Maharani," p. 42; 10″ x 12¾″.

225 "Dev Raj," p. 15, 13½″ x 9″.

226 Journey through Mourbhanj," p. 63, 13½″ x 9″.

227 "The Supper of the Holy Man," p. 86, 13½″ x 9″. (illus.)

228 Watercolor in black and red, "Pied Piper," 5½″ x 4⅜″. (possibly unpublished)

Brush and pen drawings in black watercolor illustrating *Pims: Adventures of a Dala Horse* by Skulda Vanadia Banér (New York, David McKay Co., 1964), as follows:

229 "The legs," said the hinge man, "they will have to go," p. 36, 6¾″ x 5¼″.

230 "Oh, I didn't mean all your paint!" p. 58, 6″ x 6¼″.

231 "He hops around and around," p. 133, 6¼″ x 5¼″.

232 *A Ring and a Riddle* by M. Ilin and E. Segal. Translated by Beatrice Kinkead. Illustrated by Vera Bock. Philadelphia, J. B. Lippincott, 1944.

65[10]p. 26cm. Blue cloth binding stamped in brick color. Dust jacket printed in yellow, blue, black, and rust on white.

233 Brush drawing in red and black watercolor, ". . . there on one step stood a chest," 11½″ x 8″. Illustration for *A Ring and a Riddle*. (frontispiece)

Illustrations for *Rose Fairy Book*, collected and edited by Andrew Lang (New York, Longmans, Green & Co., 1948), as follows:

234 Brush drawing in black watercolor with some red, dust jacket, 11½″ x 16¾″.

235 Watercolor overlay for dust jacket, 10¼″ x 16″.

Brush drawings in black watercolor, as follows:

236 Pictorial endpapers, 10¼″ x 14½″. (illus.)

237 ". . . he snatched up a silver tray and hastened to present the cake to the prince," p. 9, 12¼″ x 9¼″.

238 ". . . life was unbearable without her little dog," p. 21, 12¼″ x 9¼″.

239 "Bensurdatu . . . drew his sword and cut off the giant's head," 12¼″ x 9¼″.

240 ". . . a small mouse had sprung from the inside of the tureen," p. 135, 12¼″ x 9″.

241 "The path soon led to the lake of the dragons," p. 159, 12¼″ x 9¼″.

242 "I am the Lion Fairy," p. 193, 12¼″ x 9¼″. (illus.)

Brush drawings in black watercolor illustrating *Sing a Song of Seasons. Poems about Holidays, Vacation Days and Days to Go to School*, selected by Sara and John E. Brewton (New York, The Macmillan Co., [1955]), as follows:

243 Dust jacket design, 12⅛″ x 8½″.

244 "Morning is a little lass," p. 13, 9½″ x 7¼″. (illus.)

245 "Evening is a little boy," p. 25, 10″ x 7½″.

246 "Oh to have a birthday," p. 39, 10″ x 7¼″.

247 "Summer days are vacation days," p. 159, 9¼″ x 7¼″.

Illustrations for *The Tangle-Coated Horse and Other Tales; Episodes from the Fionn Saga* by Ella Young (New York, Longmans, Green & Co., 1929), as follows:

248 Black and red watercolor, dust jacket, 18½″ x 16¾″.

249 Red watercolor, pictorial endpapers, 17½″ x 24¼″.

Brush drawings in black watercolor, as follows:

250 Frontispiece, "Fionn," 16¼″ x 11″.

251 Heading to chapter "A Night of the Nights," p. 1, 15¾″ x 10¼″.

252 "In a net made of their dreams," p. 23, 15¾″ x 10½″. (illus.)

253 "Like the Jewelled Star-Dancer, Sirius," p. 33, 15¾″ x 10½″.

254 Heading to chapter "The Tangle-Coated Horse," p. 77, 6¼″ x 11″.

255 Heading to chapter "The Shining Beast," p. 96, 6¼″ x 11″.

256 "Since the king is dead," p. 103, 15¾″ x 10½″.

257 Heading to chapter "The House in the Valley of the Yew Tree," p. 108, 6¼″ x 11″.

258 "And the cold froze his eyelids," p. 145, 15¾″ x 10¼″.

259 "Riders upon White Horses," p. 165, 15¾″ x 10¼″.

260 *Twelve Great Black Cats and Other Eerie Scottish Tales* by Sorche Nic Leodhas. Illustrated by Vera Bock. New York, E. P. Dutton & Co., [1971.]

173p. 24.5cm. Red cloth binding with a cat design stamped in black. Dust jacket printed in blue and black on white.

Jean de Bosschère 1881-1953

Born in Uccle, Belgium, he lived alternately in Belgium, France, Italy and England. He was an engraver and a designer as well as a poet and a novelist. In France he became an intimate of Paul Claudel and Paul Valery. In England he formed friendships with Ezra Pound and T. S. Eliot as well as with the French-born illustrator Edmund Dulac. In 1907 he made his debut publishing books written and illustrated by himself.

261 Pen and black ink, "The Awful Tournament," 1918, 13⅛″ x 9 9/16″. (possibly unpublished.) (illus.)

262 *Christmas Tales of Flanders* illustrated by Jean de Bosschère. London, William Heinemann; New York, Dodd, Mead & Co., [1917.]

144p. 28cm. Orange cloth binding decorated in black.

263 *The City Curious* by Jean de Bosschère, illustrated by the author and retold in English by F. Tennyson Jesse. London, William Heinemann; New York, Dodd, Mead & Co. [1920.]

178 [7] p. 23cm. Gray cloth binding decorated in black and orange. (illus.)

Watercolors, possibly unpublished, as follows:

264 "The Return from the Hunt," 10¾″ x 8½″.

265 "The Young Lion Tamer," 12¼″ x 9⅝″.

Eleanor Fortescue Brickdale 1872-1945

Born in England. Daughter of a lawyer, the artist attended Crystal Palace School of Art and Royal Academy Schools in London. She worked in several art forms including design of buildings and stained glass windows as well as illustration. The first major exhibition of her art took place in 1901. For a time she taught in the art school which her friend Byam Shaw founded in 1901.

266   *Dramatis Personae & Dramatic Romances & Lyrics* by Robert Browning (Philadelphia, J. B. Lippincott; London, Chatto & Windus, 1909). 246p. 24.2cm. Gray cloth binding stamped in gold.

Lewis Jesse Bridgman   1857-1931

Born in Lawrence, Massachusetts. An etcher and illustrator who specialized in children's books.

Watercolors, possibly unpublished, 13¾″ x 10″, as follows:
267   "The Brown Centaur."
268   "The Gnome." (illus.)

Charles Livingston Bull 1874-1932

Born in Rochester, New York. He studied at the Rochester Institute of Technology and the school of art of the Corcoran Gallery, Washington, D. C. In Washington he worked as a taxidermist for the National Museum. For the U. S. Biological Survey he drew preservation posters and worked near Oradell, New Jersey, the home town of his adult life, as a reporter and surveyor. Bull was the star illustrator of Charles G. D. Roberts' nature stories, including the classic *Red Fox*. He possessed a great gift for drawing animals in action.

269   Watercolor, hawk and owl, 22¼″ x 13¼″. (possibly unpublished.) (illus.)

Clara Miller Burd

Born in New York. Pupil of Courtois and Colarossi in Paris, also studied at the Chase School and National Academy of Design in New York. In addition to illustrating children's books, she designed magazine covers, painted portraits of children, and designed and executed numerous stained glass memorial windows. She exhibited at the National Academy of Design in 1900, flourished 1911 - 1933.

270   Watercolor, two children and winged fairy gazing at book, 17½″ x 11¼″. (possibly unpublished.) (illus.)

Walter Harrison Cady   1877-1970

Born in Gardner, Massachusetts. A self-taught artist, he went to New York at the age of 18 and sold his first work — a set of decorative letters — to *True Magazine*. In 1907 he became a newspaper artist for the *Brooklyn Eagle*. Also in that year he began to draw beetles as a result of a childhood memory and sold some of these pen and ink sketches to *Life*. At 24 he joined the staff of *Life*.

271   *The Happychaps* by Carolyn Wells with illustrations by Harrison Cady. New York, The Century Co., 1908. 135p. 25cm. Light brown cloth binding stamped with pictorial design. (illus.)

John Cassel   1875-

Born in Nebraska City, Nebraska. He studied art at the Art Institute of Chicago. In New York he worked regularly for *Puck* and not so regularly for *Life* and *Judge*. He switched to book illustration and advertising. For twelve years he worked at the *New York Evening World* and then moved to the *Daily Eagle*.

272   Gouache, calf and frightened child, 14½″ x 12″. (possibly unpublished.) (illus.)

Emily Hall Chamberlin   -1916

Born in Shelby, Ohio. Studied in Paris, London, and at the Pratt Institute. She specialized in drawing children.

273   Pen and watercolor, large hand reaching down toward a small boy, 16½″ x 11¾″. (possibly unpublished.) (illus.)

Harry Clarke   1889-1931

Born in Dublin, Ireland, and educated at Belvedere College. He studied with great success at the Dublin Metropolitan School of Art and won a traveling scholarship to study early stained glass in the Ile de France in 1914. He won the only gold metals which were given at the South Kensington Exhibitions in stained glass in 1911, 1912, and 1913. He joined his father's stained glass workshop and at his father's death became managing director of the firm and principal designer. He also illustrated books published by George Harrap of London.

274 *Fairy Tales* by Hans Christian Andersen. Illustrated by Harry Clarke. London, George G. Harrap & Co., 1916.

    319p. 29cm. Vellum binding stamped in gold. Limited edition: no. 9 of 125, signed by artist.

275 *The Fairy Tales of Charles Perrault.* Illustrated by Harry Clarke with an introduction by Thomas Bodkin. London, George G. Harrap & Co., 1922.

    157p. 25.5cm. White cloth binding decorated in blue.

276 Pen, ink, pencil, and watercolor, "A long black pudding came winding and wriggling towards her," 12½" x 9⅞". Illustration, p. 130, for the tale "The Ridiculous Wishes" in *The Fairy Tales of Charles Perrault.* (illus.)

mer or The Tournament of the Rose (London, Cassell, 1891). (illus.)

278 Pencil, pen, and brown ink, "Middle of the Forest of Rosedale," 8¾" x 11¼". Illustration for Act 1, Scene 1, *The First of May: A Fairy Masque* by J. R. Wise (London, Goupil & Co., H. Southeran; Boston, Osgood, 1881.) (illus.)

Pen and watercolor illustrations for *Mother Hubbard's Picture Book* in Walter Crane's Picture Books, Vol. II, Re-Issue (London & New York, John Lane, The Bodley Head, [1896]), as follows:

279 "Mother Hubbard," 10¼" x 8½".
280 "The Three Bears," 10¼" x 8½". (illus.)
281 "The Absurd ABC," 10" x 8½".
282 Pen drawing in *Mother Hubbard's Picture Book,* advertisement for Walter Crane's Picture Books Re-Issue series, 10" x 8½".

Chalk and watercolor designs for *Pothooks and Perseverance or The ABC Serpent,* Walter Crane's New Series of Picture Books, No. 3 (London, Marcus Ward, 1886), as follows:

283 Front cover design, 8½" x 8". (illus.)
284 Back cover design, 8½" x 8".

Walter Crane   1845-1915

Born in Liverpool, son of an artist. As a lad he sketched hands and faces for his father's portraits. He studied evenings at Heatherley School of Fine Art and served as an apprentice in wood engraving under W. J. Linton. In 1862 he left Linton and — at the age of 17 — was on his own as a "pro." He worked with the color printer Edmund Evans designing covers for "railway" novels. Encouraged by Evans, he designed and drew for the inexpensive toybooks first published by Frederick Warne, then by George Routledge. His illustration of children's books was one important facet of his artist's life; he also designed wallpaper, room interiors, friezes, and tapestries. A contemporary of Kate Greenaway, Randolph Caldecott, George Bernard Shaw, William Morris, and Oscar Wilde, he moved in a circle of creative, influential people in art and politics.

277 Pen and watercolor, "And spread with 'broidered hangings gay, Till all was ready for the fray," 7¾" x 6½". Illustration for *Queen Sum-*

Marguerite Davis   1889-

Born in Quincy, Massachusetts. She attended Vassar College and the School of the Museum of Fine Arts under the guidance of William Paxton and Philip Hale. After several years of experimenting with advertising, Christmas cards, and magazine covers, she began to illustrate children's books. In 1948 she studied watercolor at the Gerry Peirce School in Tucson, Arizona. She also did illustrations for *Treasure Trails,* a children's magazine published in Chicago.

Watercolor illustrations for *Under the Lilacs* by Louisa May Alcott (Boston, Little, Brown & Co., 1928), as follows:

285 Frontispiece " 'Yes, 'm coming as fast as I can,' answered a meek voice," 18½" x 12¾".
286 "Say 'How do you do,' commanded Ben," p. 74, 20" x 12¾". (illus.)
287 "As Ben flung open the door a gray kitten walked out," p. 192, 16½" x 11⅜".
288 "Sancho scrambled out from under the seat in a great hurry to go and greet his friend," p. 152, 16" x 11".

Maurice Day 1892-

Born and grew up in Damariscotta, Maine. Studied at Massachusetts Normal Art School and Museum of Fine Arts School. In addition to illustrating children's books, Day turned his talents in art and photography to designing layouts and doing color sketches for Hollywood's cartoon studios. After five years in the film capital with the Walt Disney studio and others he returned to Maine where he now lives. Much of his time has been spent in color photography, recording the nature which he loves.

289 Pen and watercolor drawing, boy and girl planting seeds, 16½" x 12". (possibly unpublished.) (illus.)

Edward Julius Detmold
1883-1957

Born in Putney, London. He and his older twin brother, Charles Maurice, began to draw when they were five and showed such talent that their father, an electrical engineer, arranged for private education with their uncle, Dr. E. Barton Shuldham. From their studies of zoo animals and birds, and of insects, sea shells and skulls came an artistic capacity combining intense realism with fantasy and strong decorative sense. They made drawings, watercolors and etchings, and illustrated books, including a memorable portfolio (Macmillan, 1903) of scenes from Kipling's *Jungle Book*. Charles Maurice committed suicide in 1908. Edward continued as an intensely productive illustrator until 1922, when he withdrew from the world and lived as a recluse until his death 35 years later.

290 *The Arabian Nights; Tales from the Thousand and One Nights.* Illustrated by E. J. Detmold. London, Hodder & Stoughton, [1924.]

240p. 28.5cm. Vellum binding stamped in gold. Limited edition: no. 57 of 100, signed by artist.

Walt Disney 1901-1966

Born in Chicago, Illinois. Studied art through correspondence courses and at Chicago Academy of Fine Arts. Achieved recognition for his inventiveness as animator and cartoonist in cinematography. Famous for his Mickey Mouse, Donald Duck, Snow White, Bambi, and other characterizations in film.

Paintings on celluloid by Walt Disney Productions, as follows:

291 Jiminy Cricket from *Pinocchio*, 1940. 5¼" x 5".
292 Jiminy Cricket with gaily garbed female, 1940. 6¾" x 8¼".
293 Locomotive of the circus train from *Dumbo, the Circus Elephant*, 1941. 8½" x 8".

Richard Doyle 1824-1883

Born in London. He received his early training under his father, John Doyle, and in the shop of the wood engraver Joseph Swain. He joined the staff of *Punch* in 1843. In 1850 he resigned from *Punch* and began a second career as an illustrator of books. Fairy themes were his specialty, and he exhibited fairy subjects at the Royal Academy in 1868 and 1871 and at the Grosvenor Gallery before his death.

294 Watercolor, "Evil Thoughts," 7¼" x 5¾". (possibly unpublished.) (illus.)

295 *The Princess Nobody, A Tale of Fairy Land* by Andrew Lang after the drawings by Richard Doyle. Printed in colors by Edmund Evans. London, Longmans, Green & Co., [n.d.]

56p. 24.2cm. Pictorial board binding, cloth back.

Edmund Dulac 1882-1953

Born in Toulouse, France. He studied law at the University of Toulouse, attending classes at the Ecole des Beaux-Arts at the same time. Giving up his studies in law, he went to Paris and took art classes at the Academie Julian. In 1904-05 he exhibited portraits at the Paris Salon. He emigrated to England and became a British subject in 1912. He had yearly shows at the Leicester Galleries in London from 1907 to 1918. The galleries commissioned Dulac to paint a set of color illustrations for Laurence Housman's version of tales from *The Arabian Nights*, and then he began to work for Hodder and Stoughton which published the last of his Gift Books in 1918. During the 1920's he derived much of his income from portraits. During the

1930's most of his commissions were from American periodicals, and during the war years Dulac designed bank notes and stamps for the Free French.

296 Watercolor, "David and Goliath," 13½" x 11¼". Cover illustration for *American Weekly*, November 30, 1924.

297 *Edmund Dulac's Fairy Book; Fairy Tales of the Allied Nations.* New York, George H. Doran Co., [n.d.]

173p. 29cm. Black cloth binding with onlaid paper designed in black and gold.

298 *The Kingdom of the Pearl* by Leonard Rosenthal. Illustrated by Edmund Dulac. London, Nisbet & Co., [n.d.]

150p. 29.5cm. Boards stamped in silver; white cloth back. Limited edition: no. 67 of 675 copies for the British Empire.

299 *My Days with the Fairies* by Mrs. Rodolph Stawell. Illustrated by Edmund Dulac. London, Hodder & Stoughton, [1913.]

169p. 25.5cm. Red cloth binding, pictorial design stamped in gold, with added design in green and blue. (illus.)

300 *Princess Badoura: A Tale from the Arabian Nights* retold by Laurence Housman; illustrated by Edmund Dulac. London, Hodder & Stoughton, [n.d.]

113p. 29.3cm. White cloth binding, pictorial design stamped in gold, with added design in green. Limited edition: no. 98 of 750, signed by artist.

301 Watercolor, "Samson Pulls Down upon Himself and the Idolaters the Walls of Their Temple," 13¾" x 11½". Cover illustration for *American Weekly*, November 2, 1924. (illus.)

302 *Sindbad the Sailor and Other Stories from the Arabian Nights* illustrated by Edmund Dulac. London, Hodder & Stoughton, [n.d.]

221p. 29cm. Vellum binding, pictorial design stamped in gold. Limited edition: no. 49 of 500, signed by artist.

303 *Sindbad the Sailor and Other Stories from the Arabian Nights* illustrated by Edmund Dulac. London, Hodder & Stoughton, [n.d.]

221p. 28.2cm. Brown cloth binding, pictorial design stamped in gold, with added design in green.

304 *Stories from Hans Andersen* with illustrations by Edmund Dulac. London, Hodder & Stoughton, 1911.

250p. 31.5cm. Vellum binding stamped in gold. Limited edition: no. 482 of 750, signed by artist.

305 *Stories from The Arabian Nights* retold by Laurence Housman. London, Hodder & Stoughton, [1907.]

133p. 26cm. Brown cloth binding stamped in gold.

306 *Tanglewood Tales* by Nathaniel Hawthorne. Illustrated by Edmund Dulac. London, Hodder & Stoughton, [1918.]

244p. 28.5cm. Half vellum binding and boards. Limited edition: no. 488 of 500 copies, signed by artist.

307 Watercolor, circular diameter 10". Illustration for "True Spartan Hearts," a story of Beatrice Harraden in *Princess Mary's Gift Book* (London, Hodder & Stoughton, [1914.]).

Watercolors, 12½" x 9¾", possibly unpublished, as follows:

308 Oriental dancer in exotic dress. (illus.)

309 A portly, amusing ancient Greek, gaily costumed, titled "Meander" in the artist's hand.

R. Emerson

Biographical data not available.

310 Pen and ink heightened with white, Cinderella's pumpkin coach, 20" x 16½". (possibly unpublished.) (illus.)

Charles James Folkard 1878-1963

Born in London. Studied at St. John's Wood Art School and Goldsmith's Institute Art School in London. He began his career as a conjuror, then moved from magic and designing programs to writing children's plays and pantomimes and illustrating children's books. For seventeen years he contributed *Teddy Tail* for children to the *London Daily Mail*. Among the works he illustrated: *Pinocchio, Mother Goose, Grimm's Fairy Tales*.

Pen and watercolor drawings, possibly unpublished, as follows:

311 Cavorting frog-like creatures, 12¾" x 10¼".

312   . . . in woods and next to pool, 12¾″ x 10¼″. (illus.)
313   . . . with frog-like baby, 13″ x 10″.
314   . . . at a meeting, 13″ x 10″.

Henry Justice Ford   1860-1941

Born in London where he spent most of his life. He graduated from Repton and from Clare College, Cambridge. He attended the Slade School of Fine Art and the School of Art at Bushey. He was a painter and exhibited at the Royal Academy but was best known for his work as a book illustrator. In 1889 he began a long and profitable association with Andrew Lang and his wife. He did most of the illustrations and cover designs for the Coloured Fairy Book series.

315   *The Brown Fairy Book* edited by Andrew Lang with eight coloured plates and numerous illustrations by H. J. Ford. New York, Longmans, Green & Co., 1904.

    350p. 19cm. Brown cloth binding, pictorial design stamped in gold.

316   *The Green Fairy Book* edited by Andrew Lang with numerous illustrations by H. J. Ford. London, Longmans, Green, 1892.

    366p. 19cm. Green cloth binding, pictorial design stamped in gold.

317   *The Lilac Fairy Book* edited by Andrew Lang with six coloured plates and numerous illustrations by H. J. Ford. New York, Longmans, Green & Co., 1910.

    369p. 19cm. Lilac cloth binding, pictorial design stamped in gold.

318   *The Olive Fairy Book* edited by Andrew Lang with eight coloured plates and numerous illustrations by H. J. Ford. New York, Longmans, Green & Co., 1906.

    336p. 19cm. Olive cloth binding, pictorial design stamped in gold.

319   *The Orange Fairy Book* edited by Andrew Lang with eight coloured plates and numerous illustrations by H. J. Ford. New York, Longmans, Green & Co., 1906.

    358p. 19cm. Orange cloth binding, pictorial design stamped in gold.

320   *The Pink Fairy Book* edited by Andrew Lang with numerous illustrations by H. J. Ford. New York, Longmans, Green & Co., 1904.

    360p. 19cm. Pink cloth binding, pictorial design stamped in gold.

321   *The Violet Fairy Book* edited by Andrew Lang with numerous illustrations by H. J. Ford. New York, Longmans, Green & Co., 1902.

    388p. 19cm. Violet cloth binding, pictorial design stamped in gold. (illus.)

Joseph Greene Francis   1849-1930

American illustrator. Full biographical data not available.

    Pen drawings illustrating *A Book of Cheerful Cats and Other Animated Animals* (New York, Century Co., 1892) as follows:
322   "The bicycle ride," p. 15, 5″ x 7¾″. (illus.)
323   "The Prickly Pig," p. 37, 5⅝″ x 8″.
324   "The Elephant Juggler," p. 40, 6″ x 8¾″.

    Pen drawings for various issues of *St. Nicholas*, 1886-1913:
    Illustrations for "The Smallest Circus in the World" by C. F. Holder (May 1886), as follows:
325   "The hurdle race," p. 533, 4⅜″ x 8¾″.
326   "The 'go-as-you-please' race as seen through a magnifying glass," p. 534, 5½″ x 10″ (illus.)
327   "The Dance," p. 535, 5⅜″ x 7¾″.

    Illustrations in the Aztec Series, as follows:
328   "The Belated Barber — an Aztec Fragment," p. 119 (December 1887), 12″ x 9″.
329   "An Affluent Aztec — a Hieroglyphic Fragment!" p. 204 (January 1888), 12¼″ x 9¼″. (illus.)
330   "A Royal Release," p. 30 (November 1912), 10¼″ x 8″.
331   "The Jovial Judge," p. 347 (February 1913), 10½″ x 8″.

Arthur Burdett Frost   1851-1928

Born in Philadelphia. He began working in a wood engraver's establishment and later took up lithography, studying drawing during the evenings. As a chronicler of American life he was called the Mark Twain of illustrators.

    Watercolor and gouache drawings illustrating *The Story of a Bad Boy* by Thomas Bailey Aldrich (Boston, Little, Brown & Co., [1911]), as follows:

332 Frontispiece, "My Name's Tom Bailey; What's Your Name?" 14⅜″ x 9″.
333 "In the Forecastle," p. 19, 9¼″ x 8½″.
334 "A Rainy Afternoon in the Garret," p. 39, 16″ x 12½″. (illus.)
335 "Waiting for the Conflagration," p. 49, 14¼″ x 9½″.
336 "The Interrupted Celebration," p. 81, 16½″ x 10½″.
337 "The Initiation," p. 105, 16¾″ x 10⅜″. (illus.)
338 "Drifting Away," p. 169, 11¼″ x 12⅜″.
339 "Bailey's Battery Booming," p. 222, 10¼″ x 10⅜″.
340 "The Last Evening," p. 240, 8½″ x 7⅞″.
341 "Playing 'Seven Up,' " p. 267, 10¾″ x 11⅜″.

Harold Gaze

Born in New Zealand. Led a life varied in career and place. By age 10 he had traveled four times around the world. He studied art at the Byam Shaw and Vicate Cole School of Art in Kensington. In addition to his art, he studied drama and worked as an actor. During World War I he was a munitions worker. It is known that in the twenties he lived in California. He was particularly identified by his use of fairies in the backgrounds of his portraits of children.

Watercolors, possibly unpublished, as follows:
342 Mary and infant Jesus, three wise men, with side decorations of Christmas candles and angels, 12″ x 9″.
343 Mary and babe in manger, 12″ x 9¾″.
344 Three wise men above Bethlehem, 13¼″ x 10″.
345 Semi-draped female figure splashing in pool, 1929, 7¾″ x 6⅛″. (illus.)

Warwick Goble   -1943

Londoner by birth and education. After leaving school he spent several years with a printing firm learning chromolithography and commercial design. During the evenings he attended Westminster School of Art. He contributed illustrations to various newspapers and magazines before joining the staff of *The Pall Mall Gazette*. In 1893 he exhibited at the Royal Academy.

346 *The Water-Babies; A Fairy Tale for a Land-Baby* by Charles Kingsley with Illustrations by Warwick Goble. London, Macmillan & Co., Ltd, 1909.

273p. 29.2cm. Vellum binding, pictorial design stamped in gold. Limited edition of 260 copies.

John Goss   1886-

Born in Lewiston, Maine. Illustrator, painter, lithographer, teacher. In the period 1929-51 he was an instructor in and eventually headed the Department of Graphic Arts at the Rhode Island School of Design where he had studied. In 1962 he was living in Walpole, Massachusetts. He died sometime between 1964 and 1966.

Gouache drawings illustrating *Rodney, the Ranger, with Daniel Morgan on Trail and Battlefield* by John V. Lane (Boston, L. C. Page, 1911), as follows:
347 "He . . . threw [money] in the chevalier's face," 17¼″ x 11″.
348 "He bound his arms behind his back," 16½″ x 10½″. (illus.)
349 "The boy slept," 15″ x 10″.

Kate Greenaway   1846-1901

Daughter of a draughtsman and engraver residing in London. Attended the National Art Training School at South Kensington, the Heatherly School of Fine Art, and the newly founded Slade School of Fine Art. Her earliest commercial success was her contribution of several illustrations to *People's Magazine*. She first exhibited at the Royal Academy in 1877. Edmund Evans, the publisher and printer, became her patron and assured her of an ample livelihood beginning with publication of her first book, *Under the Window*. A perfectionist as a draughtsman, she was an accomplished watercolorist, recognized in a show of her own at the Fine Art Society, London, in 1891. Her designs have crisp definition and gentle colors. She conveys a sense of the quaint and old-fashioned and herself set fashions in children's dress. Her almanacs, published by Evans from 1883-1897 (omitting 1896) were immensely popular and like her other publications quickly became collector's items.

350 *The Pied Piper of Hamelin* by Robert Browning;

illustrated by Kate Greenaway. London and New York, Frederick Warne & Co., Ltd., [1910.]

48p. 25.5cm. Pictorial board binding, red cloth back.

351 *The Queen of the Pirate Isle* by Bret Harte. Illustrated by Kate Greenaway. Engraved and Printed by Edmund Evans. London, Chatto & Windus, [n.d.]

58p. 22.5cm. Light brown cloth binding printed in color.

Helen Mason Grose   1880-

She was born in Providence, Rhode Island, and spent her childhood there. She attended the Mary C. Wheeler School and the Rhode Island School of Design. She also attended the Boston Museum of Fine Arts School and the Art Students League in New York.

Watercolors illustrating *Rebecca of Sunnybrook Farm* by Kate Douglas Wiggin (Boston, Houghton Mifflin Co., [1931]), as follows:

352 Cover and frontispiece, "Mr. Cobb handed Rebecca out like a real lady passenger," 19¼" x 13". (illus.)
353 "Pink keeps clean just as nice as brown," p. 70, 19½" x 13".

Livingston Hopkins   1846-1896

American illustrator. Full biographical data not available.

Illustrations for various issues of *St. Nicholas*, as follows:
354 Black silhouette, "On the ice," p. 300 (February 1878), 3½" x 12¼". (illus.)
355 White ink on black paper with pen and black ink border simulating a school child's slate, "Slate Picture," p. 361 (March 1879), 4½" x 8½".
356 Pen drawing, "The whale smiles," 7" x 8". Illustration for "The Coral Castle" by E. T. Disosway, p. 785 (August 1880).
357 Black silhouette, "Cocquelicot expresses his opinion," 7" x 6¼". Illustration for "The Adventures of Cocquelicot" by Susan Fenimore Cooper, p. 943 (October 1881).
358 Gouache, "The dolls he made and painted were the talk of all the town," 5⅛" x 7¼". Illustration for the poem "The Conscientious Correggio Carothers," p. 679 (July 1882). (illus.)
359 Gouache, "A private rehearsal," p. 883 (September 1882), 5" x 6¾".
360 Pen drawing, "When the Mother Goose cow jumped over the moon," 8½" x 8¼". Illustration for "Hurly-Burly," nonsense rhyme by Emma Mortimer, p. 871 (September 1886). (illus.)
361 Pen drawing, "Happy-go-lucky," p. 679 (August 1897), 10¼" x 7".

Merle DeVore Johnson
1874-1934

Born in Oregon. He was the manager of the Art Department of the *New York Evening Journal* during the years 1910-1913. During 1914-1917 he was a cartoonist for *Puck*. He was well known as a bibliographer and compiler.

362 *The Remarkable Adventures of Little Boy Pip* by Philip W. Francis. The Illustrations by Merle Johnson. San Francisco and New York, Paul Elder & Co., [1907.]

60p. 22.5cm. Pictorial board binding, cloth back. (illus.)

Gertrude Alice Kay   1884-1939

Born in Alliance, Ohio. Painter, cartoonist, illustrator, Gertrude Kay studied with Howard Pyle.

Pen and watercolor drawings in orange, black, and white, 11½" x 9", illustrating *Lulu's Library* by Louisa May Alcott (Boston, Little, Brown & Co., 1930). These illustrations probably first appeared in a three-volume edition (1915-1916) from which a book of selections was published in 1930. Illustrations exhibited are as follows:
363 "The teacher was a jack-in-the-pulpit," p. 40.
364 "On came the fairy folk, making the icy world sparkle," p. 62. (illus.)
365 "Through the narrow opening two arms were stretched out to her," p. 78.
366 "The dear red umbrella flew away like a leaf," p. 92.

George F. Kerr

Biographical data not available.

Pen and wash drawings illustrating *Mother West Wind's Animal Friends* by Thornton Burgess (Boston, Little, Brown & Co., 1929), as follows:

367 "Suddenly he met Mr. Panther," frontispiece for the story "How Prickly Porky got his quills," 11¼" x 10⅜". (illus.)

368 " 'Please, please wait for me, Peter Rabbit,' panted Johnny Chuck," p. 68 for the story "How Johnny Chuck ran away," 14⅜" x 10¼".

369 " 'Come on with us to the Big River, fishing,' called Billy Mink," p. 138 for the story "Billy Mink goes dinnerless," 10¼" x 10⅜".

Pen and wash drawings illustrating *Mother West Wind's Neighbors* by Thornton Burgess (Boston, Little, Brown & Co, 1927), as follows:

370 " 'Chugarum!' began Grandfather Frog, in a very deep voice," frontispiece for the story "Why Sammy Jay cries 'Thief,' " 11⅞" x 8".

371 "Straight up to the hollow stump went Shadow the Weasel," p. 154 for the story "Who stole the eggs of Mrs. Grouse," 11" x 8".

372 "This was Peter's first snow and first Winter," p. 204 for the story "Peter Rabbit's first snow," 10⅞" x 8".

373 " 'You haven't got even common sense,' she snapped," p. 220 for the story "Mrs. Grouse goes to bed," 11" x 8".

Pen and wash drawings illustrating *Old Mother West Wind* by Thornton Burgess (Boston, Little, Brown & Co., 1928), as follows:

374 "Johnny Chuck didn't stop to think that Reddy was twice as big as he, but his eyes snapping he started for Reddy Fox," frontispiece for the story "How Reddy Fox was surprised," 11" x 12".

375 "Johnny Chuck was lost," p. 24 for the story "How Reddy Fox was surprised," 13¼" x 6¾".

376 "The door of the house was too small for Reddy Fox to squeeze in," p. 92 for the story "Peter Rabbit Plays a Joke," 14½" x 13".

377 " 'Where are you going in such a hurry, striped chipmunk?' asked Peter Rabbit. 'Down in the green meadows to find the best thing in the world,' " p. 130 for the story "Johnny Chuck finds the best thing in the world," 11" x 11¼".

378 " 'Johnny Chuck has it,' said Old Mother West Wind. 'It is being happy with the things you have and not wanting things someone else has. And it is called Con-tent-ment,' " p. 134 for the story "Johnny Chuck finds the best thing in the world," 10¼" x 11".

Thomas Mackenzie   1887-1974

Born in Bradford, Yorkshire, of Scottish parents.

He studied at Bradford College of Art and then at the Slade School of Fine Arts in London on a scholarship. When he finished his studies, James Nisbet asked him to do the watercolor illustrations for an edition of *Arthur and His Knights*. He also contributed to periodicals, especially to *The Sketch*. He left England for France but came back after the Great Depression. He died in Cornwall after a long sickness.

379 *Aladdin and His Wonderful Lamp* by Arthur Ransome; illustrated by Mackenzie. London, Nisbet & Co., [1919.]

[132]p. 33cm. White buckram binding with pictorial design stamped in gold. Limited edition: no. 241 of 250 copies, signed by the artist.

Harry Whitney McVickar 1860-

American illustrator known to have contributed extensively to *St. Nicholas* magazine. Full biographical data not available.

Pen drawings illustrating "The Frog's Tea Party" in *St. Nicholas*, June 1881, as follows:

380 "A kind invitation sent . . . ," p. 616, 8¼" x 5½". (illus.)

381 "In a minute the host in his night-gown was dressed," p. 620, 8¼" x 8½".

382 "Mrs. Frog was borne in on the arm of a guest," p. 618, 8¼" x 5½".

383 "Half-past ten struck from the great clock," p. 619, 8¼" x 5½".

Baron Ernst von Maydell 1888-1961

Painter and graphic artist born in Estonia. Studied under Purvit and at Debschitz School in Munich. Lived and worked at various times in Berchtesgaden, Munich, and Italy.

Watercolors, unpublished, as follows:

384 "The Leg-Puller," 6¼" x 7½". (illus.)

385 "The Sea Duel," 6½" x 8".

Victor Nehlig   1830-1910

Born in Paris. Studied under Cogniet. Came to

the United States in 1856 after having resided in Cuba for some time. He settled in New York. Many of his works are historical subjects.

Pen drawings illustrating the story "Dorothy's Ride" by Mrs. C. E. Cheney in *St. Nicholas*, September 1881, 12″ x 9½″, as follows:

386 Young Dorothy grips the blade of the windmill as it moves skyward. (illus.)

387 She moves higher and still higher.

John R. Neill

Illustrator and painter. Lived in New York. Illustrated many of the Oz books by L. Frank Baum and — after Baum's death in 1919 — Ruth Plumly Thompson.

388 *John Dough and the Cherub* by L. Frank Baum. Illustrated by John R. Neill. Chicago, The Reilly & Britton Co., [1906.]

314p. 23.5cm. Light brown cloth binding with pictorial design.

Peter Newell   1862-1924

Born in Illinois. Pupil of Art Students' League in New York. Much of his illustration was done for the publishing house, Harper and Brothers.

Watercolors illustrating *Mother Goose's Menagerie* by Carolyn Wells (Boston, Noyes, Platt & Co., 1901), as follows:

389 "I'm Old Mother Hubbard's Dog," p. 10, 11½″ x 8¼″. (illus.)

390 "Sure enough the wolf was weeping through one eye," p. 38, 11″ x 8¼″.

391 "The Frog who would a-wooing go," p. 70, 11″ x 8¼″.

392 Pen and wash drawing, jovial king and queen with dishpan, 10¼″ x 13½″. (possibly unpublished.)

Kay Nielsen   1886-1957

Born in Copenhagen. He was the son of famous Danish actors. He soon developed an interest in drawing and illustration and went to Paris where he attended the academies of Julian and Colarossi. He began to illustrate Heine, Verlaine, and Han Christian Andersen, among others. In 1911 he went to London where he stayed until 1916. While there Nielsen illustrated the first in a series of books due for publication in England: *In Powder and Crinoline* by Sir Arthur Quiller-Couch. In 1926 he worked in Hollywood and in 1938 he settled in Los Angeles. During this time he designed film sets and murals and also worked as an actor and director.

393 *East of the Sun and West of the Moon; Old Tales from the North* by Peter Christian Asbjørnsen. Illustrated by Kay Nielsen. [London,] Hodder & Stoughton, [1914.]

206p. 28.5cm. Green cloth binding with pictorial paper onlay.

394 *Fairy Tales* by Hans Christian Andersen. Illustrated by Kay Nielsen. London, Hodder & Stoughton, [1924.]

197p. 31.5cm. Vellum binding with pictorial designs stamped in gold. Limited edition: no. 281 of 500 copies, signed by artist.

395 *Hansel and Gretel and Other Stories* by the Brothers Grimm. Illustrated by Kay Nielsen. [London,] Hodder & Stoughton, [1925.]

275p. 30.5cm. White cloth binding, pictorial design stamped in gold, with added design in blue.

396 Watercolor and gold paint, "Snowdrop," 13¼″ x 9¾″. Illustration, p. 96, *Hansel and Gretel*. (illus.)

397 *In Powder and Crinoline, Old Fairy Tales* retold by Sir Arthur Quiller-Couch. Illustrated by Kay Nielsen. [London,] Hodder & Stoughton, [1912.]

163p. 26cm. Gray cloth binding, decorated.

398 Pen, ink, watercolor, and gold paint, "Platonic Love," 1913, 15¾″ x 7¾″. (possibly unpublished.)

399 Ink, pen, and watercolor, "The Stars," 1913, 14½″ x 9⅞″. (possibly unpublished.)

Rose O'Neill   1875-1944

Born in Nebraska. She was a self-taught artist. She went to New York where she worked for *Truth, Life, Collier's, Harper's,* and *Puck* magazines. Early in 1908 she moved to Bonniebrook, Missouri, where she originated the Kewpies, the cherubic creatures that made her famous.

Ink, pen, and brush drawings, as follows:

400 Children's Christmas party, 18″ x 22″. Illustration for *Puck*, December 4, 1901. (illus.)

401 Woman seated under a tree with girl on her lap, 21¼″ x 14½″. Illustration for C. Harper & Bro., 1904.

Frederick Burr Opper   1857-1937

Born in Madison, Ohio. At the age of nineteen he began his career as a comic artist and cartoonist with a drawing in *Wild Oats*. He drew for many publications, and his jobs included three years on the art staff of *Frank Leslie's* and eighteen years on the art staff of *Puck*. He left *Puck* to accept an offer from Hearst's *New York Journal*. Prolific as a book illustrator, in addition to his magazine and newspaper work, Opper spanned fifty-seven years in his published drawings. He retired in 1932.

Pen and ink drawings, as follows:

402 "Sir Bedivere Bors," 11½″ x 16½″. Illustration for a jingle by Frederick Burr Opper in *St. Nicholas*, October 1894, p. 1054. (illus.)

403 An armoured knight holds up a torn shirt, 12⅝″ x 16⅝″. (possibly unpublished.)

Maxfield Parrish   1870-1966

Born in Philadelphia. He studied at the Academy of Fine Arts with Howard Pyle. In 1895 he departed for Europe where he became fascinated by the pre-Raphaelites. After his return he began a richly varied career as a painter and an illustrator; he made murals for the Hotel Saint Regis in New York, designed covers for magazines, and illustrated books. With affectionate humor and imagination, he portrayed traditional characters of our folk heritage, from Old King Cole to Santa Claus. As an advertising artist, he was successful in figures and themes which became identified with major corporations. He also reached out directly to the American people; his landscapes with tranquil lakes and towering mountains and semi-classical foreground figures were accepted as a world of dream and fantasy; and millions of large color reproductions of the scenes found their way, in the years around 1920, onto the walls of American homes. Parrish's craftsmanship in drawing and color was meticulous. In 1930 he turned entirely to the painting of imaginary landscapes and dropped commercial work. He won various prizes and an honorable mention in the Paris fair of 1900.

404 Pen and ink drawing, "Edward was the stalwart, bearded figure," 7¼″ x 9½″. Illustration for story "Its Walls Were as of Jasper," by Kenneth Grahame in *Scribner's Magazine*, v. 22, August 1897. (illus.)

405 *The Knave of Hearts* by Louise Saunders with pictures by Maxfield Parrish. New York, Scribner's Sons, 1925.

46p. 35cm. Black cloth binding with pictorial paper onlay.

406 Mixed media, "The Page of Count Reynaurd," 15¼″ x 11¼″. Illustration for a story of the same title by Evaleen-Stein in *St. Nicholas*, December, 1898, p. 90. (illus.)

407 *Poems of Childhood* by Eugene Field with illustrations of Maxfield Parrish. New York, Scribner's Sons, 1914.

199p. 23.5cm. Black cloth binding with pictorial paper onlay.

Katharine Pyle   1863-1938

Born in Wilmington, Delaware. She was the sister of Howard Pyle and studied under him, at the Drexel Institute, Philadelphia, after studies at the Women's Industrial School. In a highly successful collaboration, she contributed a page of verse with pen lettering and borders introducing each of the twenty-four stories of her brother's *The Wonder Clock* (1887). She became an accomplished writer and illustrator of children's books.

408 Pen, ink, wash, and watercolor, "Her Haughty Cousins," 9″ x 12″. Illustration for her story "The Black Turkey and Her Haughty Cousins," in *Good Housekeeping* magazine, November 1912, p. 653. (illus.)

Arthur Rackham   1867-1939

Born in London; educated at the City of London School. After his visit to Australia in 1884 he entered the Lambeth School of Art. By the turn of the century Rackham had become a frequent contributor to such periodicals as *Cassell's Magazine* and *Little Folks* and began to command attention as a book illustrator. His reputation as an illustrator of colored books was assured with the publication of *Rip Van Winkle* (1905) and *Peter Pan in Kensington Gardens* (1906). Rackham exhibited his original drawings at the Leicester Galleries in London and at the Royal Watercolor Society. In 1927 he visited America and four years later traveled to Denmark and did numerous sketches for a series of illustrations for Andersen's *Fairy Tales*. Before his death he was able to complete his final illustrations for *The Wind in the Willows.*

409 *Aesop's Fables*; a new translation by U. S. Vernon Jones with an introduction by G. K. Chesterton and illustrated by Arthur Rackham. London, William Heinemann; New York, Doubleday, Page & Co., 1912.

223p. 29.4cm. Boards stamped in gold; cloth back. Limited edition: no. 1430 of 1450 copies of which 250 were reserved for USA, 200 for Australia, 1000 for Great Britain and Ireland. Signed by artist.

410 *The King of the Golden River* by John Ruskin, illustrated by Arthur Rackham. London, George Harrap, [1932.]

47p. 23cm. Decorated paper cover.

411 *The Night before Christmas* by Clement C. Moore. Illustrated by Arthur Rackham. London, George C. Harrap & Co., Ltd. [1913.]

36p. 23.2cm. Vellum binding. Limited edition: no. 147 of 275 copies.

412 *The Pied Piper of Hamelin* by Robert Browning. Illustrated by Arthur Rackham. Philadelphia, J. B. Lippincott, [n.d.]

44p. 22.3cm. Red cloth binding, pictorial paper onlay.

413 *The Sleeping Beauty* told by C. S. Evans and illustrated by Arthur Rackham. London, Heinemann; Philadelphia, Lippincott & Co., [1920.]

110p. 26cm. Decorated boards, cloth back.

414 Pen, ink, ink wash, and watercolor, "The Thirteenth Fairy," 10 3/16" x 8⅛". Illustration for *The Sleeping Beauty*. (illus.)

415 *The Tempest* by William Shakespeare, illustrated by Arthur Rackham. London, William Heinemann; New York, Doubleday, 1926.

185p. 29.4cm. Boards stamped in gold, vellum back. Limited edition: no. 68 of 520 copies, signed by artist.

416 Pen, ink, and watercolor, "There's whispering from tree to tree," 15⅛" x 10¼" from *A Dish of Apples* by Eden Phillpotts (London, Hodder & Stoughton. [1921]). (illus.)

417 *A Wonder Book* by Nathaniel Hawthorne. Illustrated by Arthur Rackham. London, Hodder & Stoughton, Ltd. [1922.]

206p. 28.5cm. White cloth binding stamped in gold. Limited edition: no. 32 of 600 copies, signed by artist.

418 Pen and watercolor, "Its three heads spluttering fire at Pegasus and his rider," 11⅝" x 11". Illustration for "The Chimaera," p. 192 in *A Wonder Book*. (illus.)

Harriet Roosevelt Richards -1932

Born in Hartford, Connecticut. Painter and illustrator. She studied at the Yale School of Fine Arts and with Frank Benson in Boston and Howard Pyle in Wilmington, Delaware.

419 Gouache, "Jamie came bouncing in with a shining morning face, a bat over his shoulder," 16¾" x 10". Illustration, p. 28, *Rose in Bloom* by Louisa May Alcott (Boston, Little, Brown & Co., 1904.) (illus.)

Charles Robinson   1870-1937

Born in London. Unlike his brother William H., he never was able to study art full time. He attended Highbury School of Art for a short period, then was apprenticed to a lithographer-printer. He studied briefly at the Royal Academy and at other schools of art. He illustrated more than a hundred books, primarily collections of fairy tales and nursery rhymes.

420 *Bee the Princess of the Dwarfs*. Retold in English by Peter Wright and illustrated by Charles Robinson. London, J. M. Dent & Sons, Ltd., 1912.

127p. 21.7cm. Gray cloth binding with pictorial designs stamped in gold.

421 *The Big Book of Fairy Tales*. Edited by Walter Jerrold and Illustrated by Charles Robinson. New York, H. M. Caldwell Co., [n.d.]

344p. 25.5cm. Red cloth binding with pictorial designs stamped in gold.

422   *Fairy Tales* from Hans Christian Andersen. Translated by E. Lucas and Illustrated by Thomas, Chas. and William Robinson. London, J. M. Dent & Co., 1899.

539p. 20.5cm. Gray cloth binding with colored pictorial design. (illus.)

423   *The Happy Prince and Other Tales* by Oscar Wilde. Illustrated by Charles Robinson. New York, G. P. Putnam, [1913.]

133p. 25cm. Blue cloth binding with pictorial design stamped in gold.

424   *King Longbeard or Annals of the Golden Dreamland; a Book of Fairy Tales*, Written by Barrington MacGregor and Illustrated by Charles Robinson. London and New York, John Lane, The Bodley Head, 1898.

262p. 20.5cm. Blue cloth binding with pictorial design stamped in gold.

425   *The Suitors of Aprille* by Norman Garstin. Illustrated by Charles Robinson. London and New York, John Lane, The Bodley Head, 1900.

211p. 19.8cm. Gray cloth binding with pictorial design in color.

426   *The True Annals of Fairy Land, Old King Cole, 1901.* Illustrated by Charles Robinson. Edited by J. M. Gibbon. London, J. M. Dent & Co., [n.d.]

338p. 19cm. Cream cloth binding with pictorial design in color.

William Heath Robinson
1872-1944

Born in London. He was trained at the Islington School of Art and at the Royal Academy Schools. He was not successful as a landscape painter and turned — like other members of his family — to illustration. His fame rests with the fantastic characters that he himself developed. He also designed theatrical scenery and created murals for the ocean liner *Empress of Britain* (1930).

427   *Bill the Minder* written and illustrated by W. Heath Robinson. London, Constable & Co., Ltd., 1912.

254p. 29cm. White boards, with pictorial design

stamped in gold. Limited edition: no. 158 of 380 copies. Signed by author/artist.

Ernest Howard Shepard
1879-1976

Born in London. Attended St. Paul's School, Heatherly's Art School, and Royal Academy Schools in London. Exhibited his first picture at the Royal Academy in 1901 and started drawing for *Punch* in 1907. During World War I he served in France, Belgium, and Italy with the Royal Artillery.

428   Pen and ink drawings surrounding poem written in script, "The Baby Tramp," 11" x 8¼". (illus.)

Sidney Herbert Sime   1867-1944

Born in Manchester, England, he worked in the coal mines of Yorkshire during his youth. He went to the Liverpool School of Art. He began to do illustrations for inexpensive comic papers. In 1895 he made his first contribution to *Pick-me-up* magazine, and this step marked the start of his career as a successful illustrator in black and white. His work began to appear in periodicals such as *The Idler*, *Eureka*, and *Pall Mall Magazine*. He illustrated Lord Dunsany's fantasy tales. In 1920 he exhibited at the St. George Gallery in London. He was not well known at the time of his death. Much of his later work is housed in the Sime Memorial Art Gallery and there is now a renewed interest in his work.

429   *Bogey Beasts; Jingles etc.* by S. H. Sime; Music by Holbrooke. London, Goodwin & Tabb Ltd., 1923.

62p. 28cm. Gray boards and cloth decorated in black.

430   Black crayon, black and gray wash, white highlighting, "By the cemetery wall, a false alarm," 19 7/16" x 13½". Illustration for the series "Ye Shades" in *Pick-me-up*, October 26, 1895. (illus.)

431   *Time and the Gods* by Lord Dunsany with ten illustrations in photogravure by S. H. Sime. London and New York, G. P. Putnam's Sons, 1922.

232p. 24cm. Half vellum and light brown cloth.

Limited edition: no. 205 of 250 copies. Autograph copy, all illustrations signed by artist.

Elmer Boyd Smith   1860-1943

Born in St. John, New Brunswick. Grew up in Boston, studied art in Paris. Much of his work as illustrator was done in Boston where he worked with Houghton Mifflin Company.

432   Gouache, scene in circus ring, 16″ x 10″. Illustration for *Circus and All About It* by E. Boyd Smith (New York, F. A. Stokes, 1909). (illus.)

Jessie Willcox Smith   1863-1935

Born in Philadelphia. Studied at the Philadelphia School of Design for Women, the Pennsylvania Academy, and the Drexel Institute. She studied under Eakins, Anschutz, and Howard Pyle — with Pyle the greatest influence on her style. She started her career as a kindergarten teacher and began her art career in the advertising department of *Ladies Home Journal.*

433   Brush, pen, and soft pencil drawing, "Howl away my painted beauties," 14¾″ x 9½″. Illustration for *The Young Puritans in Captivity* by Mary Prudence (Wells) Smith. Young Puritans Series (Boston, Little, Brown & Co., 1899). (illus.)

Alice Barber Stephens   1858-1932

Born near Salem, New Jersey. She studied wood engraving with Edward Dalziel at the Philadelphia School of Design for Women, and she was a student of Thomas Eakins at the Pennsylvania Academy of Fine Arts from 1875 to 1880. During the years 1886 and 1887 she attended the academies of Julian and Colarossi in Paris and then traveled to Italy. She began to illustrate for Harper's publications in 1887. Her "American Women Series" for *Ladies' Home Journal Magazine* secured her popularity. She illustrated for *Scribner's* and *Century* as well as illustrating many books.

434   Charcoal drawing, "Ben in Church," 19½″ x 12¼″. Illustration, p. 103, *Under the Lilacs* by Louisa May Alcott (Boston, Little, Brown & Co., 1905). (illus.)

435   Charcoal drawing, "She just tucked her cane under her arm . . . ," 17″ x 10½″. Illustration, p. 317, *Little Women* by Louisa May Alcott (Boston, Little, Brown & Co., 1902).

Arthur Szyk   1894-1951

Born in Lodz, Poland. Studied at L'Ecole des Beaux-Arts in Paris and the Academy of Cracovie. Szyk is known particularly for his revival of the art of illumination. His subjects for illustration are frequently biblical.

436   Pen and ink drawing, "Holger the Dane," 6¾″ x 5⅛″. Illustration, p. 266, *Andersen's Fairy Tales*. Illustrated Junior Library (New York, Grosset & Dunlap, 1945). (illus.)

Gustaf Tenggren   1896-1970

Born in Sweden. Studied at Valand School of Fine Arts. Illustrated children's books in Scandinavia and the U. S. where he lived until his death.

437   Watercolor, 12¾″ x 9¾″. Illustration for *Juan and Juanita* by Frances Courtenay Baylor. Riverside Bookshelf Series (Boston, Houghton Mifflin Co., 1926). (illus.)

Hugh Thomson   1860-1920

Born in Coleraine, Londonderry, Ireland. He worked in London for J. Connyns Carr, then editor of *The English Illustrated Magazine*. Between the years 1884 and 1903 he illustrated for Macmillan & Company.

438   *The Cricket on the Hearth; A Fairy Tale of Home* by Charles Dickens with seven posthumous illustrations by Hugh Thomson. [London,] The Golden Cockerel Press, 1933.

   70p. 32.5cm. Yellow cloth binding. Limited edition: no. 41 of 1500 copies.

439   Pencil and pen drawing, 13″ x 10″. Study for the illustration "Caleb Plummer and His Blind Daughter," p. 26 in *The Cricket on the Hearth*. (illus.)

440   *The Piper of Hamelin, a Fantastic Opera in Two Acts* by Robert Buchanan. With Illustrations by Hugh Thomson. London, William Heinemann, 1893.

63p. 19.5cm. Gray cloth binding, pictorial design.

William M. Timlin   1893-1943

Born in Ashington, Northumberland. He was a talented draughtsman from his early youth. He studied art at Morpeth Grammar School and won a scholarship to Armstrong College. In 1912 he followed his parents to Kimberley, South Africa. There he passed with honors the art examinations of the South Kensington Board of Education in 1914, and he founded the Art section of Kimberley's Athenaeum Club. He began exhibiting illustrations and fantasies in pen and watercolor; later he exhibited South African landscapes in etching, pastels, and oils. At the same time he was a successful practicing architect.

441   *The Ship That Sailed to Mars; A Fantasy.* Told and pictured by William M. Timlin. London, George C. Harrap & Co., Ltd., [1919.]

48p. 30.7cm. Half vellum and gray boards.

Emma Troth   -1949

American illustrator. Biographical data not available.

442   Pen drawing in black, "Pansies," 14¾″ x 10¼″. Illustration, p. 105, *Songs of Sixpence* (poems) by Abbie Farwell Brown (Boston, Houghton Miffin Co., 1914). (illus.)

Adolf Wagner   1884-

Born in Rohrbach, Austria. Studied in Vienna and exhibited statuettes and busts there from 1920 onwards.

443   Bronze statuette, "Rattenfänger von Hameln,"

["The Pied Piper of Hamelin,"] height: 18⅜″; base: 12⅞″ x 5¾″. (illus.)

Milo Kendall Winter   1888-1956

Born in Princeton, Illinois. Spent childhood in Michigan. Attended Chicago Art Institute School. A popular illustrator in the first quarter of this century, Winter preferred illustrating for children. He did a number of classics for Rand, also illustrated for Houghton Mifflin Company.

444   Watercolor, boy and girl bees standing on a flower petal, 16″ x 12″. (possibly unpublished.) (illus.)

Katherine Richardson Wireman

American illustrator. Resided in Germantown, Pennsylvania, area. Known to have been actively illustrating in 1907-14 period. She did advertising illustrations for Ivory Soap and Cream of Wheat which appeared in issues of *The American Magazine* and *McClure's Magazine.* Twenty-six years after the publication of Wiggin's *Birds' Christmas Carol* in a little fifty-cent edition Wireman illustrated a holiday edition bound in green, red, and gold. This volume — like her advertising pictures — reveals Wireman's feeling for women and children in homey settings.

Pen and watercolor drawings illustrating *Birds' Christmas Carol* by Kate Douglas Wiggin (Boston, Houghton Mifflin Co., 1925), as follows:

445   Heading and tailpiece for contents page, snow-birds, 9¾″ x 11″.
446   Invalid Carol in wicker chair, p. 17, 12½″ x 9½″.
447   Carol, leaning on crutch looking at books, p. 25, 11¼″ x 8½″.
448   Children on roof, p. 37, 8¼″ x 13½″.
449   Woman and children entering door, p. 58, 13½″ x 8¼″.
450   Larry Ruggles, caught among the umbrellas of the hat-tree, p. 72, 10½″ x 9″. (illus.)
451   Family at dining table, p. 76, 8¼″ x 13½″.
452   Girl with doll, p. 82, 11″ x 7¼″.
453   Choirboy, p. 87, 11¾″ x 7½″.

Illustrations

Boris Artzybasheff

6

13

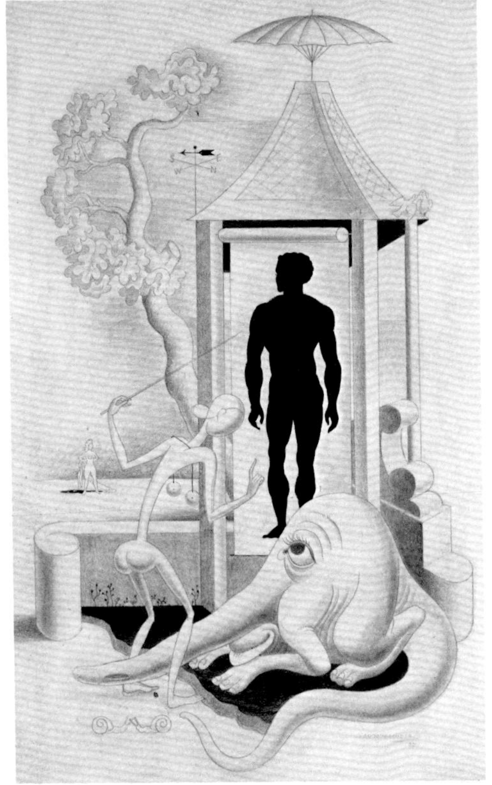

16

27

22

Boris Artzybasheff

45

48

BUFANO · MAGIC STRINGS · MACMILLAN
MAGIC
STRINGS
BY REMO BUFANO

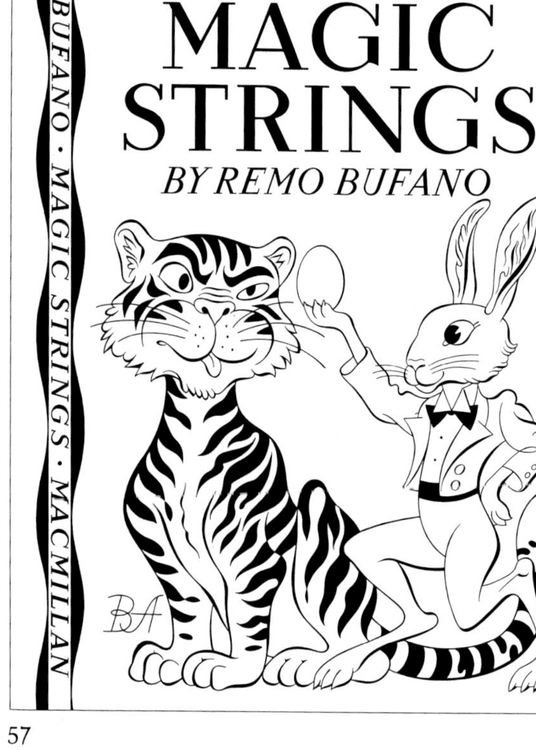

57

55

59

Boris Artzybasheff

63

44

76

68

Boris Artzybasheff

87

94

99

114 Edmund Birckhead Bensell

115 Reginald Bathurst Birch

116 Reginald Bathurst Birch

Some bold, bad thieves in a cave laughed out,
As their bags of gold they tossed;
"Sh! not so loud!" said one of the crowd;
"For if we are found, we're lost."

118 Reginald Bathurst Birch

120 Reginald Bathurst Birch

Vera Bock

131

132

136

140

149

146

164

174

170

180

Vera Bock

199

189

219

227

Vera Bock

Vera Bock

236

242

252

244

261 Jean de Bosschère

263 Jean de Bosschère

268 Lewis Jesse Bridgman

269 Charles Livingston Bull

270 Clara Miller Burd

271 Walter Harrison Cady

272 John Cassel

273 Emily Hall Chamberlin

276 Harry Clarke

277 Walter Crane

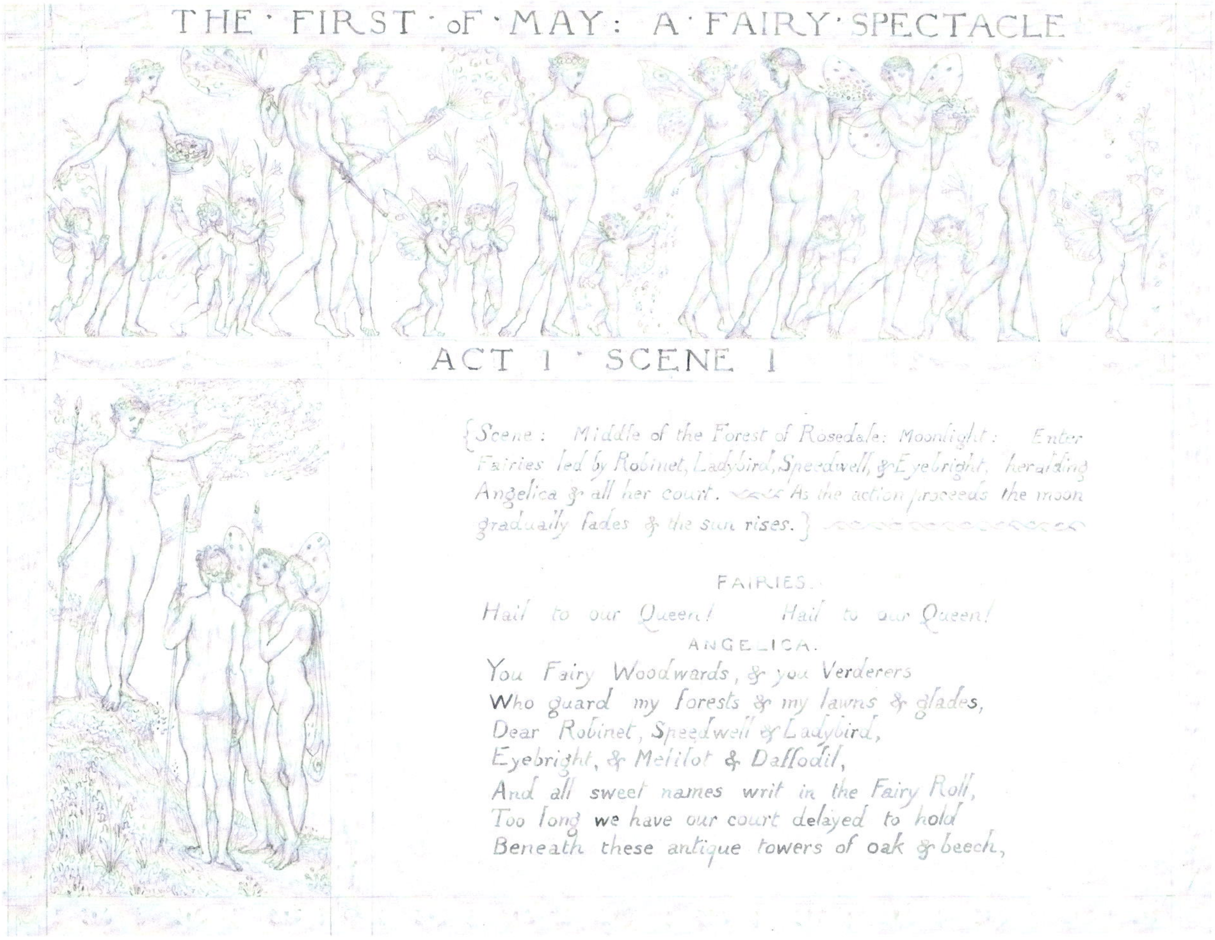

280 Walter Crane

283 Walter Crane

286 Marguerite Davis

289 Maurice Day

294 Richard Doyle

299 Edmund Dulac

301 Edmund Dulac

308 Edmund Dulac

310 R. Emerson

312 Charles James Folkard

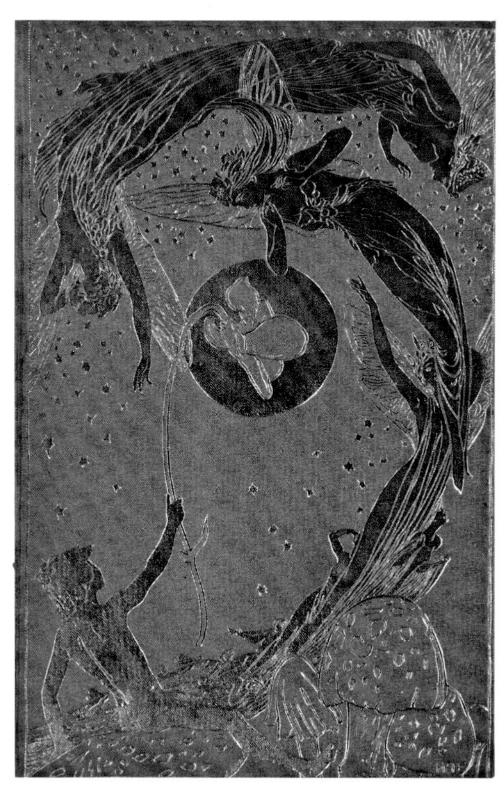

321 Henry Justice Ford

329 Joseph Greene Francis

322 Joseph Greene Francis

326 Joseph Greene Francis

334 Arthur Burdett Frost

337 Arthur Burdett Frost

345 Harold Gaze

348 John Goss

352 Helen Mason Grose

354 Livingston Hopkins

358 Livingston Hopkins

360 Livingston Hopkins

362 Merle DeVore Johnson

364 Gertrude Alice Kay

367 George F. Kerr

380 Harry Whitney McVickar

384 Baron Ernst von Maydell

386 Victor Nehlig

396 Kay Nielsen

389 Peter Newell

400 Rose O'Neill

402 Frederick Burr Opper

404 Maxfield Parrish

406 Maxfield Parrish

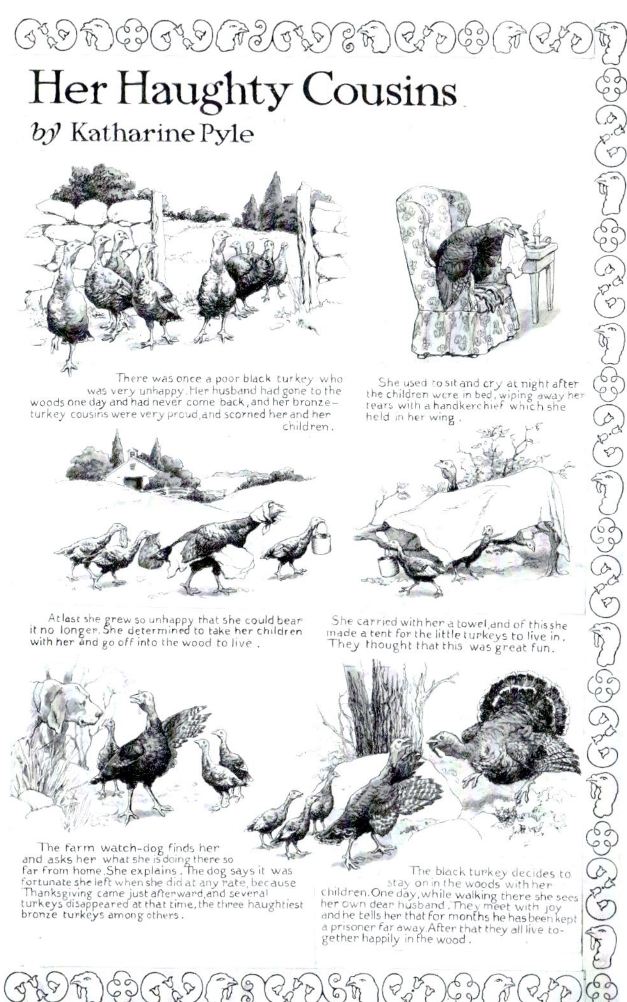

Her Haughty Cousins
by Katharine Pyle

There was once a poor black turkey who was very unhappy. Her husband had gone to the woods one day and had never come back, and her bronze-turkey cousins were very proud, and scorned her and her children.

She used to sit and cry at night after the children were in bed, wiping away her tears with a handkerchief which she held in her wing.

At last she grew so unhappy that she could bear it no longer. She determined to take her children with her and go off into the wood to live.

She carried with her a towel, and of this she made a tent for the little turkeys to live in. They thought that this was great fun.

The farm watch-dog finds her and asks her what she is doing there so far from home. She explains. The dog says it was fortunate she left when she did at any rate, because Thanksgiving came just afterward, and several turkeys disappeared at that time, the three haughtiest bronze turkeys among others.

The black turkey decides to stay on in the woods with her children. One day, while walking there she sees her own dear husband. They meet with joy and he tells her that for months he has been kept a prisoner far away. After that they all live together happily in the wood.

408 Katharine Pyle

414 Arthur Rackham

416 Arthur Rackham

418 Arthur Rackham

419 Harriet Roosevelt Richards

422 Charles Robinson

428 Ernest Howard Shepard

430 Sidney Herbert Sime

432 Elmer Boyd Smith

433 Jessie Willcox Smith

434 Alice Barber Stephens

436 Arthur Szyk

437 Gustaf Tenggren

439 Hugh Thomson

442 Emma Troth

443 Adolf Wagner

444 Milo Kendall Winter

450 Katherine Richardson Wireman